SUCCEED IN…
English

ARCTURUS

ARCTURUS

This edition published in 2012 by Arcturus Publishing Limited
26/27 Bickels Yard, 151–153 Bermondsey Street,
London SE1 3HA

ISBN: 978-1-848193-179-1
CH000724EN
Supplier 16, Date 0312, Print run 1785

Printed in Singapore

CONTENTS

CONTENTS

CONTENTS

ABOUT THIS BOOK

Success in GCSE English is vital for just about any job or course you want to pursue over the age of 16. This book will give you extra help with your GCSE English studies. It is not intended to replace the work you do in school, rather to throw a spotlight on the different parts of the examination. We will show you in detail what is required in the three aspects of the examination course: Speaking and Listening, reading and writing. We will also show you how to improve in all three areas.

All GCSE examination boards have to assess the same things but they choose to do it in different ways. Everyone starts at the same point and therefore everyone has the same opportunity. Your final grade will obviously say something about your ability but most of all it will reflect the work you have put in.

Let us be clear that there is no substitute for hard work but it is perfectly possible to work hard without being very successful. In fact, most students complain that they never seem to make progress despite working very hard. Imagine you are asked to push a car along a road. If you try pushing it sideways, you can give yourself a heart attack and not move the car an inch. If, however, you get behind the car and lean against it, the car will probably move!

Hard work alone is not the answer to success. It is focusing the work where it will be most effective that helps the student make real progress.

That is the aim of this book: to show you where to apply yourself in order to make the most of your effort.

This is not a novel. It is not designed to be read straight through from cover to cover. We have separated into sections the different aspects of GCSE English. There is a section which you will use quite frequently – Speaking and Listening – since a good percentage your final marks are awarded for the oral work you do continuously throughout the two years of the course. The section on Shakespeare will only come in useful when you are preparing for a specific controlled assessment or for an examination. The section on Spelling, Punctuation and Grammar may only seem relevant just before your written examinations.

In other words, this is a book whose various sections will be needed at different stages and different times to suit your studies: a sort of dictionary of GCSE English.

In each of the areas, we:

● explain what has to be done for the examination
● suggest ways to make the most of your efforts
● offer different levels of achievement and show you how you can improve your grades
● give examiners' tips based on examiners' reports on GCSE English

Finally, you have shown how serious you are about doing well by purchasing this book. May we wish you every success!

WRITING TO ARGUE, PERSUADE OR INSTRUCT

In GCSE English you are asked to produce a variety of writing styles in order to demonstrate your all-round ability as a writer. These used to be arranged in what are called triplets and it is still relevant to look at them in this way. The first of these is Writing to Argue, Persuade or Instruct. The other two styles are covered in the following two sections.

You will find examples of different levels of achievement in each of the styles and advice on how to improve your grades. Each triplet starts with a definition to show you what is involved.

Here, as everywhere in this book, we shall consider three levels of performance:

3 Competent – candidates who achieve the required standard
2 Good – candidates who display confidence and a deeper understanding
1 High Level – candidates who give excellent responses and show impressive skills

TRIPLET ONE: ARGUE, PERSUADE OR INSTRUCT

You have to show evidence of your ability to do three things:

- To develop logical arguments and support them with evidence
- To use persuasive techniques and employ devices that convince your reader
- To anticipate your reader's response, deal with opposing arguments, use language to interest and hold your reader's attention

Writing to argue

This is a fairly straightforward activity. You are asked to present a case on a subject about which there are opposing points of view. The question will always be framed in such a way as to indicate that an argument needs to be presented. For instance, you will not find a title such as, 'What are your views on the death penalty for murderers?' It is more likely to be phrased, 'Do you agree that murderers should be sentenced to death?'

Remember, you are not going to be marked for your opinions – the examiners will know all the arguments in any case – but for the way you organise and express them.

Get into the habit of using a method when you are tackling this sort of title.

1. If you have any choice, **select a subject that interests you** and on which you can write from personal experience. It is quite easy to write about whether or not school uniform is a good idea since you need not do a great deal of research. On the other hand, an essay about the desirability or otherwise of genetically modified food is likely to be hard work from the word go!

2. On a blank sheet of paper, **write down any idea** that comes into your head about the subject. Don't organise it at this stage, just let the ideas come to you.

3. Now draw a line down the page dividing it in half. At the top of one side write Pros and put Cons on the other side. **Organise your arguments** so that opposing views are side by side.

4. Make notes beside the ideas to **show the evidence** that supports the argument.

WRITING TO ARGUE, PERSUADE OR INSTRUCT

Organising your ideas

You are ready to begin!

Essay title:

Is school uniform a good idea?

Let's follow the advice and note a few ideas:

Gives school a recognisable identity
All students wear the same so there is no competition
Is invariably unattractive
Lots of arguments with teachers about what you can wear
Everybody hates having to wear it
Many adult occupations require a uniform to be worn
Some students are proud of their uniform
It's a cheaper alternative for parents
Look in any clothes shop – fashion has its own uniform
Some items, like blazers, are very expensive
Schools have shops selling second-hand uniforms
Wearing a tie is uncomfortable
Many civilised countries don't have school uniforms
Uniforms do not allow students to be individuals

Now organise the material into separate lists:

Examiner's Tip
Everything you write on the exam paper is marked – even if you cross it out!
This is just in case you have crossed out something that the examiner thinks is important. Always make a plan: it shows you are organising your work.

- *Gives school a recognisable identity*
- *All students wear the same so there is no competition*
- *Many adult occupations require a uniform to be worn*
- *Some students are proud of their uniform*
- *It's a cheaper alternative for parents*
- *Look in any clothes shop – fashion has its own uniform*
- *Schools have shops selling second-hand uniforms*

Pros

Cons

- *Is invariably unattractive*
- *Lots of arguments with teachers about what you can wear*
- *Everybody hates having to wear it*
- *Some items, like blazers, are very expensive*
- *Wearing a tie is uncomfortable*
- *Many civilised countries don't have school uniforms*
- *Uniforms do not allow students to be individuals*

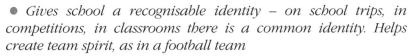

Adding the evidence

WRITING TO ARGUE, PERSUADE OR INSTRUCT

Now add the evidence:

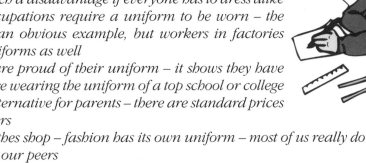

- *Gives school a recognisable identity – on school trips, in competitions, in classrooms there is a common identity. Helps create team spirit, as in a football team*
- *All students wear the same so there is no competition – poorer pupils are not at such a disadvantage if everyone has to dress alike*
- *Many adult occupations require a uniform to be worn – the armed forces are an obvious example, but workers in factories and shops have uniforms as well*
- *Some students are proud of their uniform – it shows they have done well, if they are wearing the uniform of a top school or college*
- *It's a cheaper alternative for parents – there are standard prices from school outfitters*
- *Look in any clothes shop – fashion has its own uniform – most of us really do not like to look different from our peers*
- *Schools have shops selling second-hand uniforms – this sensibly recycles uniforms at a price that makes them affordable*

Pros

Cons

- *Is invariably unattractive – pupils do not get a choice, and fashion changes while school uniforms remain the same*
- *Lots of arguments with teachers about what you can wear – stupid regulations cause a lot of trouble: girls wearing trousers; shirts having to be tucked in; particular shoes being required etc*
- *Everybody hates having to wear it – you are branded from the moment you leave home to the moment you get back; it never looks nice*

- *Some items, like blazers, are very expensive – apart from the cost, they cannot be worn out of school unless you want to appear a complete fool*
- *Wearing a tie is uncomfortable – in the twenty-first century who wants to wear a tie apart from bank managers and civil servants?*
- *Many civilised countries don't have school uniforms – go to France, the USA or Canada and they don't have school uniforms. Are they all stupid?*
- *Uniforms do not allow students to be individuals – they take no account of personal tastes and you often end up never wanting to wear that colour or combination of colours ever again*

Now look at the way a candidate might write the essay:

3   Competent

The candidate will probably be happy just to set out the argument and make sure that it is covered. Whenever this book refers to a candidate, it is taken for granted that 'he' or 'she' will apply equally. No sex discrimination is ever implied!

The opening of a typical essay might go something like this:

'School uniform is a very argumentative subject. Lots of people have different opinions, for and against. I am in favour of it and I hope that this essay will show you why I think it is a good thing…'

Comment

The reader can challenge none of this though the word, 'argumentative', is a little weak. A person might be called argumentative whilst an issue like this might better be described as contentious. The second sentence makes complete sense but it is so obvious that it is hardly worth stating!

2   Good

'School uniform is one of the things that will always make young people hot under the collar! Nearly all schools in Great Britain insist that it should be worn and the one I attend is no exception.'

Comment

This paragraph says much the same as the previous candidate's effort but is altogether more confident in its use of language: notice expressions like 'hot under the collar' and the more adult vocabulary of 'insist'; and 'the one I attend' instead of 'my school'. The reader has not been told where the writer's sympathies lie so there is a chance that the reader's interest will be engaged while waiting to see where the writer is going.

1   High Level

'"The uniform 'e wore
Was nothin' much before
An' rather less than 'arf of that behind"

Thus Rudyard Kipling describes the uniform of the courageous water-carrier Gunga Din. Fortunately, the same could not be said of most school uniforms, all of which specify the right colour of trousers or skirt, shirt or blouse, and even a cap and blazer in some instances. Schools lay down the rules – and the student puts them on in the morning. But should schools have the right to insist on their students attending classes in a particular set of clothes?'

Comment

If the Good candidate showed confidence, then the High Level writer is positively bursting with it! She has taken the trouble to find a quotation that relates to the topic. More importantly it is slightly humorous, so we start the essay with a smile. There is an extra quality here – that the writer appears to be quite well-read. Moreover, the paragraph ends with a question. What better way is there to involve your reader than by asking him a direct question?

The closing paragraph:

3   Competent

'I hope I have shown you the different sides of the argument. I don't think people will ever agree on this subject and will always find something wrong with it.'

Comment
This is quite a bald ending. The writer concludes as she has begun – by stating the obvious. The language is quite simple and the writer bids us farewell with a bland sentence.

2   Good

'Students will probably always object to being told what to wear by teachers. You can hardly blame us, especially when we look at the clothes that our teachers wear! I mean, let's face it, what qualifications does a man in a tweed jacket with leather elbow patches have when it comes to clothes?'

Comment
This is an enjoyable way to sign off. The argument about school uniform is never going to be decided and this writer admits that, whilst poking a little gentle fun at her style gurus – her teachers! The closing question effectively leaves the reader thinking about what has been said.

1   High Level

'Like Gunga Din many students are surprisingly happy to wear school uniform. They may not be especially courageous in doing so but it is on the whole quite a practical solution to what young people should be wearing in the white heat of battle at school!'

Comment
You know the writer has reached the end of her essay since she is returning to the point she made at the beginning. This  *is a clever way of getting your writing to hang together. It also allows her to make one or two last humorous comments, not so much about teachers as about the nature of education, and should leave the reader thinking.*

WRITING TO ARGUE, PERSUADE OR INSTRUCT

Top tips for progress

- Plan your answer

- Think of an original way to begin

- Use questions to engage your reader

- Develop the argument logically

- Don't be afraid to make your reader smile

- Don't give away your opinions until the very last paragraph

- Balance the arguments

Writing to persuade

'I flew to LA (for) a couple of days with friends…At the car rental office the clerk hoped I'd had a great flight, offered me a cup of tea, loved my accent, and just had to let me know that I could upgrade to a convertible for so few more dollars it was a steal. "You'd really see LA better with the top down," he added.' (Professor Miles Robbins, Compass Magazine Wessex)

We see persuasion everywhere. People and organisations spend long hours and a great deal of money trying to convince others to agree to a point of view or a course of action. The car rental clerk spent time winning Professor Robbins' friendship and trust in order to make a little extra money. Professor Robbins saw through this as you can tell from his expression, the clerk *'just had to let me know'*, as if the clerk could not resist indulging in a little bit of salesmanship. The Professor saw through it – would you?

You may not end up working in car rentals but throughout your life you will be trying to persuade other people to see things your way. Just as importantly, you too will be on the receiving end more often than not. Whilst we may work out how to persuade others for our benefit (and theirs, we hope!), we need to understand the techniques for ourselves if we are not to spend our lives being manipulated by everyone else.

The four guiding principles

When you write to persuade, remember four guiding principles:

- Use persuasive techniques
- Employ devices that convince your reader
- Anticipate arguments that your reader may bring up
- Address your reader as YOU

Essay title:

Persuade a friend that his views on animal rights are wrong

This time we shall make notes on the arguments your friend gives as to why he is in favour of animal rights

Notes

- Animals have the same rights as humans
- Animals have feelings and intelligence
- They are entitled to happiness just as we are
- There are plenty of ways of testing drugs without using animals
- Factory farming is cruel
- There are alternative ways of handling livestock that allow them freedom
- We don't need to eat meat
- Hunting animals is cruel
- Zoos cruelly cage wild animals
- We don't need animal furs since there are plenty of man-made alternatives
- We shouldn't use animals in sport

WRITING TO ARGUE, PERSUADE OR INSTRUCT

Examples of different levels of achievement

3   Competent

'I agree that animals have feelings like you and me but we are the bosses on the earth. If they were in charge, would they look after us? I don't think so.

I hate eating greens and there's lots of people like me. They couldn't just eat veggies all the time so we have to have meat. And zoos are useful because we can see what wild animals are like without having to go abroad to see them.

You can't get rid of hunting animals. A fox will just go into a bunch of chickens and kill the lot, even if he doesn't want to eat them. Bullfighting isn't very nice but the Spaniards like it so good luck to them I say. Don't be cruel to animals but we are in charge.'

Comment *This has all the points you would need and they are expressed in a lively way. The use of paragraphs shows the writer has prepared her essay and is aiming for a structure but there is no evidence to support her arguments at all. The language is not very convincing. Don't be afraid to stretch your vocabulary. Someone who 'just eats veggies all the time' is a vegetarian. Expressions like, 'we are the bosses' and 'a bunch of chickens' are very slangy. There is no convincing start or finish. The weak language, the lack of evidence and the brevity all combine to put this in the competent category.*

2   Good

'Human beings are the dominant force on earth. That is a fact of life and it is down to human beings to look after animals in the way that best suits them.

You may be right that we do not need to eat meat but it does supply certain things which would be hard to find in other foods. Things like protein are a vital part of a human's diet and it is meat that supplies it. I am not saying that vegetarians are wrong, just that I could not survive on what they eat. Me – I just love steak and chips. Don't you?

It is easy to say that hunting is cruel. On the face of it, a cuddly little fox being chased across fields by a red-faced bugle-blowing brigade of cavalry is (a) not much of a match and (b) a very cruel thing, but does cuddly Mr Fox worry about the chickens he kills for the fun of it? We need chickens and we don't need foxes. So, let's hunt them down.

Bullfighting could be seen as a cruel sport and we don't have it in our country but the bull is treated with respect by the matador and by the spectators. It may not be a pretty sight for English visitors but that is the way they do things in Spain and I do not think you have the right to tell Spaniards how to live their lives.

Personally I love animals – I have a cat and a couple of pet snakes, so don't talk to me about cruelty to animals. I treat them with love and make sure they are happy and well-fed. That is the way we should treat animals and I don't think there's any need to go on animal rights marches to prove it!'

Comment *This is clearly a stronger piece of writing. For a start it has a weightier feel to it. The writer is not afraid to use the language by showing a varied vocabulary – words like 'protein', 'dominant' and 'spectators' – and by devising the occasional humorous phrase – 'cuddly Mr Fox' and 'red-faced bugle-blowing brigade'. Overall this is a good read but the really good candidate would be weighing the arguments a little more carefully and producing the stronger ones. Finally, as the objective was to get someone to change their point of view, we would expect rather more persuasion to be used.*

1 High Level

'I cannot believe that a person as intelligent as you actually believes that there is such a strong case for animal rights. Surely the facts speak for themselves.

The human species is not just a naked ape. We are altogether different from the rest of the animal kingdom. We have the power of thought and the ability not just to communicate our ideas but to write them down and have them preserved for posterity. Thus we do not learn from our peers but from humanity through the ages.

We are omnivores: many dinosaurs were herbivores, lions are carnivores. Our diet is far more varied. Down the ages we have learnt how to farm, not just crops and vegetables but also animals, which we use for our welfare. Yes, we kill animals and eat their meat but our talents extend beyond that. We use the wool from sheep for our clothing, the milk from cows for a wide variety of tasty dishes and even harvest eggs from chickens for our benefit.

But we are cleverer than that. Our scientists have learnt how we may protect our species by developing medicines and countless preparations that we use in everyday life. We have learnt how to test those products before we allow human beings to use them. Occasionally, this means that animals have to die for our benefit but only because our first duty as a species is to protect and preserve ourselves.

Animals do not have the same rights as human beings, if only because human beings have responsibilities and duties. The law protects us but in return we have to obey the law for everyone's sake. We may get hungry but no one would ever suggest that we eat each other as animals do.

Bullfighting is one of those things that is very hard to defend but I am not a Spaniard so I can only guess at their enthusiasm for it. There is so much ceremony surrounding the spectacle that it is plain they have great respect for the bull. It is treated with reverence and the matador is regarded as a great and valiant fighter. The bull has his hour of glory and then like every other bull is slaughtered for human consumption. Right or wrong? I cannot tell. Without it though we should never have had that glorious song 'Toreador'. The world would be a poorer place without that!

The world is not perfect, of course, but we must constantly strive towards perfection and work within the law to ensure that all people are safeguarded. There are still so many millions of people living and dying in poverty that our first duty is always towards them. Only when we have made humanity safe can we afford the luxury of extending the same protection to all animals.

How can you, a civilised teenager, disagree with that?'

Comment *The first thing you notice is that this is a much more wide-ranging piece of writing. The paragraphs are linked together so that you feel the writer is developing her argument. Sentences like, 'But we are cleverer than that', help to join the ideas together and suggest that the writer is anticipating what her friend might be thinking. The vocabulary is more sophisticated: we kill cattle for food becomes 'slaughtered for human consumption' because the writer is treating the reader as an intelligent person. Above all there is a confidence in this writing, and if the writing is confident there is far more likelihood that the persuasion will be taken seriously.*

WRITING TO ARGUE, PERSUADE OR INSTRUCT

Top tips for progress

- Believe in what you want to say

- Organise your ideas

- Anticipate your reader's questions

- Use a personal style to convey your ideas: it is 'I' speaking to 'you'

- Use colourful language to put across your points

- Use questions to involve your reader

Writing to instruct

This form of writing is quite tricky. It is concerned with conveying information in such a way that the reader can carry out what you are telling him to do. The secret of good instructive writing is to concentrate on the task in hand. There is no room for ambiguity or diversion.

Imagine a radio presenter is dictating the telephone number of his show to a phone-in audience. The commonest tactic he will use is to write it down at the same time as he is giving it to his audience. In that way, he knows that the average listener will have ample time to get the number right. It is that sort of thinking that should guide you when you are producing instructions. If you cannot do what you are asking, then you cannot expect your reader to do it either!

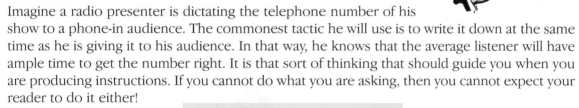

Planning the writing

Use this approach when you are planning the writing:

- Write down the stages by which you reach the desired ending
- Keep instructions short. Don't say, 'Next you do…' Instead say, 'Do this…now do that…' and so on
- Use concise, clear sentences
- Employ the exact vocabulary

Example

Essay title:

Produce instructions showing how to set your Sky+ to record a programme from an iPhone

Your mum has called you in a panic. She is out for the day and has forgotton to set the Sky+ box to record Eastenders. She wants you to email her instuctions to record remotely.

Get the Sky+ App

First you need good internet connection. Find the blue App Store icon on your iPhone homepage. Click on it (ie. touch it) and you should then see five icons at the bottom of the screen. Click on the Search icon, – a magnifying glass – and type in Sky+. Make sure you use the + key and not the word 'plus'. It should come up as the first App in the search results. Click on it and then click the blue tab that says 'FREE'. It will turn green and will say 'INSTALL'. Click on this and type in your password. The App should start downloading to your phone.

WRITING TO ARGUE, PERSUADE OR INSTRUCT

Using the App

Click on the new Sky+ icon on your phone. As this is the first time you have used it, you will be asked to enter your Sky Username and Password. Your username is tracey.needham and your password is Daniel31. You will not have to do this again.

Finding the programme

You should now be looking at a screen that has three options at the top – Showcase, TV Guide and Search. If you want to see what is on and when, you should click on TV Guide, but for *Eastenders*, click on Search and enter 'Eastenders' into the box. It will then give you a list of all the *Eastenders* episodes on this week, including those on BBC HD and BBC Three. Click on the one you want to record.

Check the details

The screen will give you the date and time the episode is scheduled to broadcast, along with a brief description of the episode. If it is the one you want to record, click on the red RECORD tab at the top right of the screen.

Record once or the series

It should ask you whether you want to record only this programme or if you want to record the whole series. If you never want to forget again, click on 'Record series'. If you only want to record this episode, click on 'Record once'.

Done!

You should now see a 'Record' icon appear by the date and time. It is a white 'R' in a red circle. If you can see it, then the Sky+ box at home is now set to record. You can click 'Done' in the top left and quit out of the App. If you can't see it, you probably haven't touched the 'Record' button properly. Try again and it should work.

The only flaw in the plan is if someone at home has turned the Sky+ box off at the plug, or if they override your remote command. You might want to call Dad and Dan, just to make sure!

Comment

The information has been laid out for ease of reference using paragraph headings that refer to what the user will see on the phone screen. The language is simple since the user is not skilled in the use of smart phones. If she was, she would not need the instructions!

Top tips for progress

- Think before you write

- Identify the different stages of the instructions

- Use simple user-friendly English

- Keep sentences short

- Work on layout to improve understanding

- Try your instructions yourself or with a friend

- The quality of an instruction depends on the clarity of its organisation

Writing to argue, persuade or instruct

WRITING TO INFORM, EXPLAIN AND DESCRIBE

TRIPLET TWO: INFORM, EXPLAIN AND DESCRIBE
This style of writing shows your ability:

- To form sentences and paragraphs that express how information and ideas are related by such things as making comparisons, or by showing how one thing causes something else
- To use formal English and accurate expression
- To anticipate what the reader wants to know and supply relevant details
- To present material clearly, using appropriate presentational devices such as statistics and illustrations

Writing to inform and explain

When you write to instruct, your reader has to listen to you. You do not have to make any effort to interest him: if he does not do what you say, he will be sunk! Your writing has to be to the point at all times and concentrate solely on the task.

When you write to inform, your reader does not have to listen at all but you feel that there is something he ought to know, so you have to:

- Make the information relevant to the reader
- Make it interesting to keep the reader on your side
- Go for straightforward sentences

Read this information on the death penalty that appeared on the Amnesty International website (www.amnesty.org) in 2003 and answer the questions below it.

Abolitionist and Retentionist Countries
Over half the countries in the world have now abolished the death penalty, making a total of **111** countries.

Eighty-four other countries **retain** and use the death penalty, but the number of countries that actually execute prisoners in any one year is much smaller.

Death Sentences and Executions
During 2001, at least **3,048** prisoners were executed in **31** countries and **5,265** people were sentenced to death in **69** countries. These figures include only cases known to Amnesty International; the true figures are certainly higher.

In 2001, **90 per cent** of all known executions took place in China, Iran, Saudi Arabia and the USA. In China, the limited and incomplete records available to Amnesty International at the end of the year indicated that at least **2,468** people were executed, but the true figure was believed to be much higher. At least **139** executions were carried out in Iran. In Saudi Arabia, **79** executions were reported, but the total may have been much higher. **Sixty-six** people were executed in the USA.

The Deterrence Argument
Scientific studies have consistently failed to find convincing evidence that the death penalty deters crime more effectively than other punishments.

Effect of Abolition on Crime Rates
Recent crime figures from abolitionist countries fail to show that abolition has harmful effects. In Canada, the homicide rate per 100,000 population fell from a peak of **3.09** in 1975, the year before the abolition of the death penalty for murder, to **2.41** in 1980, and since then it has declined further. In 1999, 23 years after abolition, the homicide rate was **1.76** per 100,000 population, **43 per cent** lower than in 1975. The total number of homicides reported in the country fell in 1999 for the third year in a row.

Execution of the Innocent

As long as the death penalty is maintained, the risk of executing the innocent can never be eliminated.

Since 1973, **102** prisoners have been released from death row in the USA after evidence emerged of their innocence of the crimes for which they were sentenced to death. Some had come close to execution after spending many years under sentence of death. Recurring features in their cases include prosecutorial or police misconduct; the use of unreliable witness testimony, physical evidence, or confessions; and inadequate defence representation. Other US prisoners have gone to their deaths despite serious doubts over their guilt.

The Governor of the US state of Illinois, George Ryan, declared a moratorium on executions in January 2000. His decision followed the exoneration of the **13th** death row prisoner found to have been wrongfully convicted in the state since the USA reinstated the death penalty in 1977. During the same period, **12** other Illinois prisoners had been executed.

Announcing the moratorium, Governor Ryan said: 'I cannot support a system which, in its administration, has proven so fraught with error and has come so close to the ultimate nightmare, the state's taking of innocent life... Until I can be sure that everyone sentenced to death in Illinois is truly guilty, until I can be sure with moral certainty that no innocent man or woman is facing a lethal injection, no one will meet that fate.'

The Death Penalty in the USA

- The use of the death penalty was resumed in 1977
- **71** prisoners were executed in the USA in 2002
- Over **3,700** prisoners were under sentence of death as of 1 January 2002
- **38** of the 50 US states provide for the death penalty in law

Questions

1. What is the worldwide attitude towards the death penalty?
2. What is the picture according to the statistics in:
   - China?
   - the USA?
3. Is this article written in favour of the death penalty or against it?
4. Give your response to what this article says.

Suggested notes for your answers

1. More countries (111) do not use the death penalty than do (84). The trend appears to be downwards with fewer people being executed.

2. China is very strict with the death penalty – 2,468 being executed in a single year, compared with 66 in the USA. The USA reintroduced capital punishment in 1977 and has many in death row awaiting execution but the Americans are worried about mistakes! The suspension of the death penalty in Illinois shows this.

3. The fact that it appears on the Amnesty International website would suggest that it is anti the death penalty. The information given shows that the number of countries using the death penalty is falling and the article does not say that this is a bad thing! It also has sections looking at the deterrent effect of the death penalty and the effect of abolition on crime rates. Both sections suggest that the death penalty does not deter violent crime and, where it has been abolished, it seems that fewer murders are taking place.

4. You may feel that the article is too one-sided. It comes from Amnesty International so they are bound to be against the death sentence. The inconvenient facts are that it does not appear to work and the figures look pretty convincing. You might say that does not bother you because you think murderers should be put to death. You still need to answer the question posed by the Governor of Illinois – can you accept that some people who are executed are innocent? If you can, and you will need to explain why you do not mind innocent people dying, then your case in favour of the death penalty is complete.

The ability to write a letter is one we all need, especially when we are writing to inform.

Laying out the address

There are two equally correct ways of punctuating an address on an envelope:

Miss Amelia Wright
1 Leafy Avenue
Chorlton-cum-Hardy
MANCHESTER
M13 4AA

Miss Amelia Wright,
1 Leafy Avenue,
Chorlton-cum-Hardy,
MANCHESTER.
M13 4AA

The choice is yours: either use no punctuation, or put a comma at the end of every line and a full stop after the town/city name. Always print the post-town and the postcode in BLOCK CAPITALS!

Laying out a business letter

Different companies have different styles and the layout of a business letter is often affected by the company notepaper and how it is headed. The layout on the next page is perfectly satisfactory, though you need to be prepared to adapt your style to suit your employer should you opt for working in an office!

WRITING TO INFORM, EXPLAIN AND DESCRIBE

The business letter

ROYAL THEATRE The Royal Theatre, Scotland's Best Writing Theatre, is seeking an experienced, full time

PRODUCTION MANAGER

For full application pack please send a SAE to Pauleen Rimmer, Royal Theatre, Wellington Street, EDINBURGH EH1 3ED
Closing Date: Fri 3 February 2012, 6pm
The Royal Theatre is an equal opportunities employer

1 Leafy Avenue
Chorlton-cum-Hardy
Manchester
M13 4AA

Pauleen Rimmer
Royal Theatre
Wellington Street
Edinburgh
EH1 3ED

24 January, 2012

Dear Ms Rimmer,

Application pack for Production Manager vacancy

I was interested to read in today's *Guardian* that you have a vacancy for a Production Manager.

Would you send me a full application pack? I enclose a stamped addressed envelope and look forward to hearing from you.

Yours sincerely,

A. Wright

Amelia Wright (Miss)

Amelia is writing to the Royal Theatre asking for an application pack.

Comment

- *Having put Pauleen Rimmer's name at the top of the company's address, it is difficult to know how to address her at the top of the letter*
- *You could say 'Dear Pauleen' but that is too informal – it sounds as if you already know her. You could write 'Dear Pauleen Rimmer' but that is a little clumsy. If the original advert had her title as Mrs, Miss or Ms, that would have been straightforward. The only sensible option you have is to settle for the female title that does not describe her marital status. And you may well ask yourself why women should have to declare whether or not they are married when a man can be plain Mr and you cannot tell if he is available or not!*

Another possibility is to start the letter, 'Dear Madam', though this title does not go down well with some women! However, some women don't like 'Ms' either, so you pays your money as they say and takes your choice!
- *It is helpful to put a heading at the top of the letter so that Ms Rimmer can see immediately that this is a letter requesting the application pack*

- *Tell her where you saw the advertisement so that she knows that it was worth advertising there and so that she knows exactly what you have read in connection with the vacancy*
- *Write only what is essential – you might give your right arm for this job but now is not the place to say that*
- *Generally speaking, a letter beginning 'Dear Sir' or 'Dear Madam' ends with 'Yours faithfully'. 'Yours sincerely' is saved for people whose names you know, whom you may address as 'Dear Mr…' or 'Dear Mrs/Miss/Ms'. In this case, although you do not know your addressee, you do have her name, so use 'Yours sincerely'.*
- *Put your name beneath your signature and add the title by which you wish to be known*

The Curriculum Vitae or CV

WRITING TO INFORM, EXPLAIN AND DESCRIBE

This is a Latin phrase that means the story of your life. As with so many things, there is not just one right way of presenting a CV (plural CVs) but you won't go far wrong if you adopt the style of the CV below for your own.

Comment

This gives the most general idea of Amelia's life story: it shows where she grew up, what qualifications she obtained and what she did with them. There is a year unaccounted for in this CV – did you spot it, and can you guess what she did? I think it may have been a gap year when she travelled the world in search of herself, only to discover that she had been a teacher all along! Sad story, eh?

CURRICULUM VITAE

Name:	Miss Amelia Justine WRIGHT
Address:	1 Leafy Avenue, Chorlton-cum-Hardy, Manchester M13 4AA
Education:	1985–1991 – St Anne's Infant and Junior School, Morecambe, Lancs 1991–1998 – Masterson's College, Exeter, Devon 1998–2002 – Exeter University, Devon
Qualifications:	GCSEs: English (A*), English Literature (A*), Mathematics (B), Chemistry (A), Physics (B), French (B), PE (C), Geography (A), Drama (A) A levels: English (A), French (B), Geography (B) Degree: BA Hons English (upper second) Postgraduate qualifications: Teaching diploma
Work:	2003–present: English teacher at the Eton Comprehensive, Manchester M13
Achievements:	Produced school plays, edited school magazine, managed school library, leading roles in Chorlton Thespians
Interests:	Reading, playing chess, writing, voluntary work
Referees:	Mrs Longman MA Eton Comprehensive School Manchester M13 4BB Head Teacher Mrs T H Hardy Masterson's College Exeter Head Teacher

The CV also provides prospective employers with the names and addresses of people whom they may contact in order to find out how good Amelia really is.

WRITING TO INFORM, EXPLAIN AND DESCRIBE

Writing for a reference

One of the things you will need when you are applying for a job is a reference from someone in a position of authority who can tell the world what a marvellous person you are! Don't ask your mother to do this. She will naturally support your personal belief that you are the best thing since sliced bread but in general employers think that mothers tend to be a little biased. The same applies to your next-door neighbours, the man in the corner shop and the milkman.

In other words, for your referees you need people who are not personally involved in your life and who have some standing in the community.

The obvious person to approach is your last head teacher. Such a letter may look like this:

> 1 Leafy Avenue
> Chorlton-cum-Hardy
> Manchester
> M13 4AA
>
> Mrs T H Hardy
> Head Teacher
> Masterson's College
> Exeter
> Devon
> EX4 3DT
>
> 28 January, 2012
>
> Dear Mrs Hardy,
>
> <u>Amelia Wright (née Watson): September 1991 – June 1998</u>
>
> I am currently applying for the post of Production Manager at the Royal Theatre, Edinburgh, and I would be grateful if I could use your name as a referee in my application.
>
> I left Masterson's in June 1998 with three A levels and 9 GCSEs. My tutor group teacher for most of the time was Mr Ahmed.
>
> As you know, I went to Exeter University where I did an English degree and qualified as a teacher. Now I am at the Eton Comprehensive School, Manchester, teaching English and Drama. Much as I love teaching, I think the time has come for me to take a chance in the professional theatre.
>
> I hope you and all at Masterson's are well and I would be grateful if you would convey my best wishes to Miss Baxter, who was such an inspirational drama teacher. I am sure she would be pleased to hear that her good work has made at least one of her ex-pupils crazy about going on the stage.
>
> Yours sincerely,
>
> *A. Wright*
>
> Amelia Wright

Comment

- *The writer identifies herself so that the head teacher can easily find her in the school records*
- *She has married since leaving school so includes her maiden name which will be on the records*
- *Describing her qualifications makes it easier for Mrs Hardy to complete a reference*
- *A friendly note makes the head more interested in helping Amelia*
- *Identifying a teacher who knows her, helps the head to get a fuller picture for the reference*

Letters of complaint

WRITING TO INFORM, EXPLAIN AND DESCRIBE

There are often occasions when we have cause to complain about goods or services. We may enjoy having a good old moan about something but usually we only bother to write and complain if we feel we can get something back. We need to be quite systematic with such correspondence and *try to remain as polite as possible*.

This extract from a longer letter is quite effective.

I would like to draw your attention to the following complaint about the accommodation your company provided us with at Hotel Juliet, Bennazi, Venice, from July 10th – 17th this year.

Our room was arguably the shabbiest room I have ever had the misfortune to spend time in. We complained immediately to our representative, Fatima Toogood, but she was unable to organise a move for us to anywhere other than the Hotel Shack. Since that was awarded two stars by your ratings and since the move there would cost us upwards of a hundred pounds, we felt disinclined to take the offer.

The room was small. The furniture consisted of a chipped wardrobe; a low desk, also chipped; twin beds whose mattresses did not fit their bases so it was impossible to sit up in any comfort to read; and the mattresses themselves were so hard that our backs ached for most of each day.

There was a balcony. However, since it was on the south side of the building and gave no shade from the fierce sun, it was useless.

The shower was in a dark and cramped room. It had a single 'window' which was just a space bricked in with earthquake bricks and a further window which was opened and closed by means of a dirty rag affixed to a metal catch of some description. The bathroom wall itself was so thin that every sound made by the people next door was clearly audible...

Comment

- *Do not directly insult the company – icy humour is much more effective*
- *Be as accurate as you can with the details that you think are worthy of complaint*

Letter of complaint about goods

Once again, it is important to be polite and accurate. There is nothing to be gained from upsetting the recipient.

15 Carter Street
Barnet
Hertfordshire
EN1 4WW

The Manager
The Sweater Shop
14 Boulevard Avenue
Manchester
M15 6AS

Dear Sir,   2 February, 2012

Return of sweater

I enclose a sweater which I ordered from your company on 21.12.11. I am afraid that you have sent me the wrong size and it is far too large for me. I would be grateful if you would return the money I paid.

Yours faithfully,

Comment

- *The use of a heading makes it clear what the letter concerns*
- *Supplying the date makes reference to records straightforward*
- *The customer is very clear about what action is required*

WRITING TO INFORM, EXPLAIN AND DESCRIBE

Writing to explain

When you write to explain, it is like drawing the curtains back and letting in daylight: you are making everything clear. What is more, because the writing is intended to make everything clear it has to stand on its own. This means you need to:

- Structure the writing so that everything fits together
- Keep to the facts
- Define the technical terms

Essay title:

Explain why it is hard to learn English spelling

The playwright, George Bernard Shaw (1856–1950), always wrote in Pitman's shorthand which was then transcribed by his secretary. He felt too much time was wasted on English spelling and campaigned for a new alphabet. The simplified alphabet that he proposed consisted of 40 letters grouped into four types: shorts, talls, deeps and compounds. Surprisingly, it never took off!

Our complicated spelling stems from a variety of causes. The Anglo-Saxon alphabet had 24 letters to convey 40 basic sounds. After 1066, French scribes respelled much of the language, for example introducing qu- for cw- and gh- for h-. Then many of the early English printers were foreign and they had their own ideas about spelling. Moreover, after the Elizabethan age all manner of loan words joined our vocabulary, leading to yet more variety in spelling.

Famous sentences such as 'Though the rough cough and hiccough plough me through, I ought to cross the lough' give the impression that English spelling is chaotic. Yet less than 25 per cent of words are spelt irregularly and only three per cent are so unpredictable that they have to be learnt by heart. Unfortunately, many of the most frequently used words are the irregular ones.

Comment

This is tailored to the task. The introductory paragraph explains Shaw's attitude towards writing: it was a simple matter of conveying ideas and having to worry about spelling was a waste of his time. Pitman's shorthand system uses strokes, crosses and circles to represent sounds of words. His attempts to simplify spelling succeeded only in making it more complicated. The writer picks up the idea of complication and applies it to the reasons behind our 'complicated spelling'. A quick dash through history gives us an overview of what happened to our language, and the writer ends by cheering us up – it's not really that difficult!

Top tips for progress

- **Compose a clear introduction**
- **Use simple literal English to inform**
- **Use technical English in explanations**
- **Use straightforward sentences**
- **Lay out with care to help your reader**
- **Include facts and figures**
- **Read it to a friend to check it makes sense**

Writing to describe

Here at last you can let your imagination off the lead and allow it to wander freely round the park, sniffing at bushes, snuffling through leaves and even stopping at a telegraph pole…But enough, gentle reader, let us not let our imaginations run completely riot!

Some people love descriptive writing. They positively revel in the freedom it gives them. Frankly, you either like it or hate it – there seems to be no halfway house here but remember these guidelines if you are trying it for the first time:

- Your writing is much richer if you use lots of comparisons and figurative language
- Your sentences will be freer
- Your vocabulary is stretched to its limits

Examples of different levels of achievement

Essay title: *Describe your favourite place*

3	**Competent**

'My favourite place is a place I take my dog to not far from my house. It is up a hill and you have to park your car in a car park which is often where there are robberies so you have to be careful. When you walk up the hill, you can see for miles right across to Andover. There are fields everywhere and it all looks so green.

At the top of the hill is a stack of trees which are all over the place and the walk is around the old fort walls which are made of earth. It is ever so big and my dog loves it though he often runs off and I can't find him.

It takes about half an hour to walk all the way round and when you get back to the car you are hoping you have not been robbed!'

Comment

This conveys some information – the writer likes going to a hill somewhere which has trees and a car park! The language is very generalised and a bit too informal in tone: 'stacks of trees' and 'ever so big' do not exactly grab the reader. It has a lively ending which links in with the overall description but frankly it seems a bit too worrying a location to merit the title, 'My favourite place'!

31

2   Good

'One of my favourite places is Danebury Ring just outside Andover. It is an Iron Age hill fort and archaeological excavations by Professor Barry Cunliffe of Southampton University have revealed that it was a very thriving community three thousand years ago.

Today the hill is a large overgrown area with trees and bushes where humans once lived. You will see the traces of the excavations in a clearing and find chalk circles where Iron Age man stored his grain.

Above all, it is a peaceful place. It covers such a large area that you can disappear and fancy yourself back in time, miles from anywhere and simply enjoy the solitude. It has been carefully cared for by preservation societies and is home to a wide variety of wild flowers, some very rare orchids amongst them, and a dazzling array of various song birds.

Just to wander there of an afternoon with my dog makes me so contented. It's a place where you can be alone with yourself and your thoughts.'

Comment

The writing is much more precise. The writer takes pains to point out the history of the place and to add details that bring the place alive for the reader. There is some effective description but really this essay could just as easily be entitled: 'A historical site' – it is not obviously a favourite place. On the credit side, the writer does avoid mentioning the fear of car thefts!

1   High Level

'Favourite places always have a special quality. They bring out something uniquely important to the individual. They may be observation spots that have beautiful views or locations with a thrilling atmosphere.

My choice is rather an odd one for a young person I think. I do not care for crowds; I prefer somewhere secluded where I am safe and alone. A place where my mind is engaged with the surroundings yet I can reflect upon the world and its problems.

Such a place is Danebury Ring, an Iron Age hill fort, rising out of the beautiful Hampshire countryside not far from the London overspill town of Andover and the rather more grand Stockbridge, where Lillie Langtry used to spend nights with Edward VII. It is an important archaeological site but that is a small part of its attraction for me.

I say 'small' because I like to be somewhere that has a sense of history but civilisation has long since departed, leaving earth ramparts which enclose the woods and crown the hill as the only sign that once this was a bustling village.

The vastness of the place is what I like. I can feel buried inside the ramparts and the twentieth century is a million miles away. You see hardly anyone there and on a hot summer's afternoon, you can lie in the long grass and shut your eyes and feel at one with the natural world.

A magical place indeed.'

Comment

Notice the writer is standing back from the subject to start with. She makes us think about our own favourite places and suggests that what she feels is what we feel too. In this way we are involved from the start. We have no idea of the location of the favourite place. This is a writer who is trying to convey the quality of the place. In this way, she leads us into an understanding of why this is such an important place.

Notice how the paragraphs are carefully stitched together giving the writing a natural feel and a sense of organisation, as though the writer is leading us through the place. The link between Paragraph 2 and Paragraph 3 shows you how to do this. The writer is talking about places where her mind is 'engaged with the surroundings…' She begins Paragraph 3 with the expression, 'Such a place', linking the ideas and pushing the description along.

The confident vocabulary and word pictures help us to realise the quality of the writing and the short closing paragraph neatly and effectively sums it all up.

Top tips for progress

- **Always plan before you start writing**

- **Refer back to your plan as you write to avoid wandering off the point**

- **Work out each sentence in your head before you write it down**

- **Make the layout as clear as possible to help your reader**

- **Use paragraphs to indicate the structure of your writing**

- **As you write, think about the questions your reader might want to ask**

- **Stretch your vocabulary at all times**

- **Check your work afterwards to eliminate errors**

WRITING TO IMAGINE, EXPLORE OR ENTERTAIN

TRIPLET THREE: IMAGINE, EXPLORE OR ENTERTAIN

This is probably the most rewarding of all forms of writing since it is more personal in nature than any other style.

You have to be able:

- To draw on your own experience of reading prose and/or poetry, and watching or performing in plays
- To use language imaginatively and employ different literary techniques
- To shape your language and organise your writing so as to achieve different effects to appeal to your reader
- To use your knowledge of language to convey ideas, themes and characters

Though three forms of writing are included in this section, there is no point in giving different examples since they can all be classified as original writing.

How original writing is assessed

Since original writing can take so many different forms, it is hard to tailor the advice just for you. Let's see what the examiners are looking for at the different levels – and how we can improve our work.

3 Competent

Throughout this book, Competent means the standard required to achieve a GCSE pass. All GCSE syllabuses show what is required but syllabuses are designed for your teachers so the language they use is not always easy for candidates to understand. We shall interpret the grade criteria and give some examples so that you can see for yourself where you can make key improvements.

There are several features that the Competent candidate displays:

- *The writing usually matches style and form to purpose and audience*

The crucial word here is **usually**. The reader feels that the candidate is making some sort of an effort to **tell a story in an interesting way**.

- *The writing begins to make use of sentence structures and vocabulary to create effects*

The key phrase here is **begins to make use**. The candidate is trying to **do something different**.

- *Spelling of irregular words is generally accurate and punctuation helps to clarify the meaning*

The candidate is attempting to use **more difficult expressions** and realises that **punctuation is used to help convey the meaning**.

- *The writer constructs well-plotted narrative, including detailed ideas and descriptions*

A well-plotted narrative is **a story that is planned** and is reasonably **developed**.

2 Good

At this level the candidate is aware that she is writing for an audience at all times.

- Candidates' writing is coherent and controlled
- There is a range of sentence structures and a variety of vocabulary to create effects and engage and sustain the reader's interest
- Paragraphs, accurate spelling and punctuation make the meaning clear
- Work is presented attractively
- The candidates give powerful accounts of real or imagined experiences

The Russian playwright Anton Chekov was a notable critic as well as being a successful dramatist. One of his observations about staging a play is particularly relevant to the work of a Good candidate:

'If there is a gun on the wall in the first act, it will be fired in the fifth act!'

Works of art do not just happen. As the term suggests, they have to be worked at. Think of the photographer: his task is to create a picture by omitting anything that might distract the viewer from the essential subject. If he is producing a portrait of a beautiful woman, he would make absolutely certain that she is not posed before a tree that appears to be growing out of her head! He will compose the picture in the lens before pressing the shutter button.

Remember Chekov's words when you are trying to make your writing coherent. Coherence, by the way, is the quality that a work of art possesses: everything hangs together beautifully.

With an artist it is a different matter entirely. He starts with a blank sheet of paper, and he chooses what he will include. His portrait of the beautiful woman will certainly not have a tree growing out of her head!

The writer's craft is very close to that of the artist. There should be nothing in your writing that you do not want, and what is in your writing should be conveyed in the very best language at your disposal in order to make the picture as clear as possible.

The first thing you must do is plan your writing as carefully as you can in the time available. This will enable you to put the gun on the wall, which you will later be able to fire. This also gives the reader a sense of achievement since he will be able to say, 'How clever. I spotted that!' And if you can make the reader feel clever, he will certainly feel that you are a clever writer!

Planning must include paragraphing. Look back to the Competent candidate – no mention there of paragraphs. That's because the Competent writer is not aware of the effects that you can create with paragraphs.

The final attribute of a Good candidate is that his writing is **powerful**. Simply put, this means that the reader is moved by the writing.

Power in writing is achieved through **choice of the right word to describe the right detail** but above all you gain it through **concentrating on the task**, reliving it, as it were, for the benefit of the reader.

1 High Level

The best writing accounts for the top sixteen per cent of all candidates, with just over a quarter of those attaining the most prized of all the grades – the A*. For an examiner this writing very often provokes amazement. It is even more astonishing when you take the age of the writer into consideration.

The grade criteria suggest the following qualities:

- Candidates' writing is elaborate or concise, vigorous or restrained as appropriate
- It employs a wide vocabulary and a precise fluent style which is technically almost faultless
- It consciously shapes and crafts language to achieve sophisticated effects

Examiner's Tip
Paragraph your work – it shows you are structuring your answers.

What the highest level candidates have is an enjoyment in writing that communicates itself to the reader. The accuracy of the language enables the writer to reconstruct experience in such a way that the reader is never distracted by irritating lapses of expression, or punctuation or spelling.

WRITING TO IMAGINE, EXPLORE OR ENTERTAIN

Examples of different levels of achievement

In this section we shall look at three candidates' attempts at the same essay title to show you how to improve your writing.

Preparing a special meal: Candidate 1

'For my Mum's treat this year's Mother's Day, I volunteered to make the Sunday dinner.

First I got her a bunch of flowers and took it up to her bedroom along with a cup of coffee and her favourite scrambled eggs and smoked salmon on toast. Then I left her with dad and the colour supplement and went downstairs to make the dinner.

I decided that we should have roast beef with all the trimmings. Mum loves Yorkshire puddings and thick gravy and scrumptious roast potatoes, a perfect treat when you are being spoilt.

I laid the table with the best tablecloth and set out the best cutlery with a vase of daffodils I had picked from the garden. It looked a real treat.

Then I peeled the potatoes and partly boiled them before putting them into the roasting dish along with the beef. I peeled some carrots and chopped up a spring cabbage and got them ready for boiling when the meat was nearly cooked.

When it was all ready and I had done the Yorkshires, I carved the joint and put the slices on the plates and laid them on the table. We had a smashing meal and Mum just loved it.

It was my way of thanking her for all the love she has given me over the year.'

Comment

This is short but it succeeds in recapturing some of the enjoyment of preparing a meal for a special person.

The writer is beginning to use language for effect: look at the fourth paragraph which describes the table in a long sentence and follows it with a short sentence. The writer also gives some evidence that she is trying to tell a story: this has a beginning, a middle and ends with an appropriate comment.

Overall, it is a reasonable reconstruction of an event but the writer never really lets herself go. This is Competent writing.

Preparing a special meal: Candidate 2

'Don't you just love Mother's Day?

It gives you the chance to repay a little of the huge debt of gratitude you owe your Mum. People have all sorts of ways of doing this but the way I always favour is to give her a day off housework and all the normal chores.

The centrepiece of the day is Sunday lunch. Our family loves sitting down on a Sunday to a lovely old-fashioned Roast Beef dinner: succulent meat, crispy roast potatoes, vegetables fresh from the garden and, of course, light puffy Yorkshire puddings. We always have them the proper Yorkshire way (because Mum is a Yorkshire woman), that is, separately with gravy before the main meal.

I always lay the table with special care. Normally we might eat Sunday lunch on our knees in front of the omnibus edition of *EastEnders* but Mother's Day is special so it has to be the best tablecloth (a white damask one which was Mum's grandmother's), the best crockery (a delicate Wedgwood china set, also inherited) and the best silver cutlery. This year I complete the effect with a bouquet of spring flowers from the garden and an expensive bottle of red wine.

It is pleasant to have the kitchen to myself – I can hear Mum upstairs listening to *Desert Island Discs* as she luxuriates in a nice hot bath, whilst downstairs I am peeling potatoes, and chopping vegetables, and mixing up the batter for the Yorkshires. The beef is washed and put into the oven and the countdown begins. The trouble with me is that I tend to cook things too early and on too high a temperature so that you know it's ready when the smoke alarm goes off!

Finally all is done – the potatoes and meat and vegetables are in the warming drawer and the Yorkshires are ready to emerge from the hot oven. The gravy is ready and it remains for me to open that bottle of red wine and put it on the table.

This year there has been no smoke alarm so I simply call upstairs to Mum, Dad and my brothers that dinner is ready.

I go out to the kitchen to fetch the Yorkshire puddings and when I return, Mum is sitting there looking at the flowers and the table. Her eyes are filled with tears…'

Comment

The writer has taken considerable care with this piece: words are carefully selected; descriptions are not hurried. We feel we are really there on that Mother's Day.

It is little details that give this writing its authenticity. The family watch EastEnders, *they have great-grandmother's tablecloth, there is a garden outside with spring flowers in it. There is humour, too, as the smoke alarm going off is a very common experience for the amateur cook. The story ends with a contrast, summing up all the mixed emotions of a mother on this special occasion.*

All in all, this piece of writing definitely deserves a Good grade.

Preparing a special meal: Candidate 3

'I settled on a meal of salmon rolls stuffed with crab and lobster, mashed potatoes, peas, julienned carrots and parsnips and a hollandaise sauce to spread over the salmon rolls, with a honey and mustard sauce on the carrots and parsnips. A splendid banquet preceded by tarasamalata, a tzatziki dip with a variety of cheeses, breads and crackers. The meal would then conclude with a birthday cake and champagne.

The dinner was set for 7.30 pm so I shopped in the morning and started my preparations around 4.30 pm. First I peeled the potatoes using a completely new peeler. It seemed to work wonderfully well and I found myself removing outer skins at lightning speed. Somewhere around speed number four, I took a small chunk out of the index finger of my left hand. It bled but little and I was soon able to patch it up and continue. But with a little less in the speed department and a lot more in the care.

As a result I lost some time.

Somewhere around five, I commenced julienning the carrots and parsnips – always a time-consuming process. However, recently I purchased a remarkable new device for thinly slicing vegetables, part of a wonderful Japanese plot to rid the world of occidentals whilst significantly increasing its GNP.

This superb piece of kitchen-aid is a flat surface like a cribbage board with a sharp knife sticking up in the middle and all one has to do is move a couple of screws to adjust the cutting height of the blade. I estimated I needed about 1/4 inch slices after which I would cut them lengthways with one of my nicely sharpened but old-fashioned knives.

I took the first, quite large, carrot in my right hand and drew it along the cutting board. The first slice was perfect. So easy and so quick. I realised I would soon make up the time lost on the potatoes. I went at the slicing with renewed vigour, rapidly working my way through the innocent carrot.

Then suddenly a rather sharp pain introduced itself into the top of the small finger of my right hand. This was followed by an excessive amount of blood spreading over the nicely polished cutting surface.

Maintaining my usual presence of mind, I turned on the cold water tap and placed my finger under it, discovering fairly soon that I had sliced a quarter of an inch off the top. It hung rather dejectedly in the cascade of cold water and the blood showed no inclination of ceasing its bubbling flow even after several minutes.

So I took a chunk of ice, placed it on the cut and then wrapped a tea towel very tightly, first around the pinkie, no longer so pink, then around the next finger and then around the whole hand. Remembering my first aid in Boy Scouts I carried the hand high and waited for the sanguine flow to cease. Soon the tea towel had become saturated and I had to get a new one.

On removing the first towel and returning the little finger to the water, I noticed that I had also chopped into the next finger (or, rather, the Japanese had planned to remove two fingers with one stroke) and now I needed rather more ice with the second towel. Blood rapidly appeared through this next towel so I realised that my experiment with julienning, to say nothing of the preparation of the entire meal had come to a premature end.

In the end I was able to phone a friend to do all the work while I instructed with my right hand held high in the time-honoured salute to kamikaze pilots. I have discovered that the real difference between the professional chef and the amateur cook is in their uniforms and bearing. Where the chef wears a white hat and a long white coat and carries his head high, the cook makes do with a cheap hairnet, a crimson apron, hands covered with elastoplasts and bandages, and a decidedly hangdog expression as his right hand leans against his ear.'

Comment

This is an example of the very best writing. It is original and highly entertaining. The reader sits back and doesn't want it to end.

One of its striking qualities is the way it creates its own world: the julienne device is Japanese and the writer exploits the connection in a witty way, leaving the reader with a picture of the amateur cook covered in blood and saluting the kamikaze pilots. The early mention of julienne carrots and parsnips helps to give the writing coherence: we little realise until the writer begins to prepare those vegetables how important this feature of his meal is destined to be.

This deserves the highest grade because of its command of language. The scene can be clearly visualised and the original humour makes this memorable.

How to tell a good story

Task: *Write about an incident that was very important in your life*

This is a very common subject and a very tempting one. It enables you to draw on your own experience and allows you complete freedom to expand in any way you wish.

● Choose an incident that stands out for a particular reason. The most likely reason is that the incident taught you something about yourself or other people that you had not realised before

● Before you start writing think what it was that you realised. This might seem very obvious but many candidates simply start writing about an event they enjoyed or hated and they do not raise their heads from the paper until they have finished

● Knowing what it was that you realised shapes the entire story. If it was that you discovered a new interest, or that you understood that there are different ways of bringing up children, or whatever, that is the point where you should start the writing

Let us imagine that one Christmas Day you suddenly realised there was much more enjoyment in giving presents than in receiving them.

The structure of the average Christmas Day will give you the plan for your essay. It will eventually centre upon presents and the ritual you observe in your home.

Examples of different levels of achievement

3 — Competent

The Competent candidate might well start the story:

'I woke up at 7.30 and listened to the sounds of church bells. Being a lazy person I always lie in bed for as long as I can before I get up. Eventually the sound of my little brother shouting with delight in his bedroom forced me out of sleep and I decided to get up…'

Comment

This is a fair enough way to begin a description of a Christmas Day but the reader has no clue what to expect other than the story of this writer's Christmas Day. If you think that the story is predictable, the chances are that you will lose interest by the time the writer has decided to get up.

2 — Good

A Good candidate will immediately focus on the interesting aspect of the title: the incident.

'It was the sound of my brother playing with his new toys that forced me out of bed that Christmas morning. I am normally very slow to get up even on Christmas Day but the sound really affected me…'

Comment

Immediately this is more pointed than the first story's beginning since the writer is – for some reason – drawing our attention to the brother playing with new toys. Why that should be so important is what will make this story interesting.

1 — High Level

A High Level candidate will often start somewhere else than in bed on Christmas morning for he is not interested in Christmas presents themselves, rather any presents at any time.

'Have you ever been given a present that you desperately wanted? And found that when you actually unwrapped it, you weren't really all that bothered about it? Life is full of anticlimaxes like that.

The one pleasure that presents do give is enjoyment – the enjoyment of watching someone unwrap something you have chosen for them. I don't think I ever realised that until one Christmas morning a few years back…'

Comment

Notice that once you have started on this track, the rest follows quite easily. The real work in writing is the thinking that is done before you start, which enables you to find just the right opening.

Story-telling: the narrator

WRITING TO IMAGINE, EXPLORE OR ENTERTAIN

There are a number of ways in which you can tell a story:

● The most obvious is for you to be telling the story yourself – *a first person narrative*. This has the advantage of allowing you to speak directly to your reader but it is limiting since you can only talk from your own viewpoint. There is a way round this and that is by having a person telling you what he has overheard other people saying or seen others doing

● Another approach is to write in *the third person*. This way the reader can see everything that is happening and the writer can move you from place to place at will. This is the technique used in film-making where the camera moves us around like gods being able to see everything

Examiner's Tip
If you are writing to entertain, choose an entertaining subject!

● Another way of writing is to write *as though you are in the mind of a character*:

'Mr Baxter watched the boys on the playing field for a long time, staring intently. They were up to something but exactly what he couldn't figure out. Then it dawned on him…they were practising parts for the pantomime he was putting on. How astonishing that his class had been so keen on performing…'

This is as limiting in its way as telling a story in the first person but the difference is that the reader imagines he is superior to the narrator and knows better!

● James Joyce in his wild novel, *Ulysses*, explored a different style of narration, known as the 'stream of consciousness', as if the writer is speaking aloud what he is thinking or doing

'Mr Leopold Bloom ate with relish the inner organs of beasts and fowls. He liked thick giblet soup, nutty gizzards, a stuffed roast heart, liverslices fried with crustcrumbs, fried hencod's roes. Most of all he liked grilled mutton kidneys which gave to his palate a fine tang of faintly scented urine.'

Mmm, nice!

(Ulysses)

Script writing

Always look for different ways of entertaining your readers. Writing a play script is worth considering if only because you can use it twice: once as a piece of original writing and, secondly, as a script for Speaking and Listening coursework.

The difficulty of using dialogue in an ordinary story is that:

● It slows down the story
● It is difficult to punctuate correctly
● It is hard to judge how much you need

But if you have an ear for speech, you probably enjoy composing dialogue so scripting a play is an interesting avenue to explore.

Study the opening of this play:

Act One
(As we hear the musical introduction for the first song, we see LES, the Lollipop man, enter. He is very old, almost blind and can hardly walk. A group of KIDS, on their way to school, enter, shouting 'Hia Les,' 'All right there Les,' and singing.)

KIDS: We're goin' out
           Just for the day
           Goin' off somewhere far away
           Out to the country
           Maybe to the sea
           Me Mam says I can go…if it's free

(During verse two the KIDS exit singing and CAROL enters also singing.)

CAROL: The sky is blue
KIDS: The sun's gonna shine
           Better hurry up 'cos it's nearly nine
           This is the day that's
           Just for us
           We're goin' out…on a bus

(Carol is about to make her way to the school when she notices Les on the other side of the road.)

CAROL: Hia Les.
LES   *(trying to see)*: Who's that?
CAROL *(crossing to him)*: Carol, it's Carol, Les.
LES: Hello love. 'Ey, can y' see me back across the road? *(As she takes his arm and leads him back.)* You're early today aren't y'?
CAROL: Yeh. We're goin' out. On a trip.
LES: Where to?
CAROL: I dunno. It's somewhere far away. I forget.
LES: Are they all goin'?
CAROL: Only the kids in the Progress Class.
LES: The what?
CAROL: Don't y' know what the Progress Class is? It's Mrs Kay's class. Y' go down there in the week if y' can't do reading or sums or writing. If you're backward like.
LES: By Christ, I'll bet she's kept busy. They're all bloody backward round here.

(Our Day Out by Willy Russell)

Comment

The play starts with a burst of life as the Kids enter. They greet Les, the Lollipop man, and start singing. Carol joins in and continues the conversation with Les when the rest have gone. We do not need any description of the setting: this is obviously outside a school where there is a crossing attendant. The lighting needs no explanation since the characters comment on the sun shining in a blue sky. The meaning of the play's title is immediately apparent.

A play script observes certain rules:

- The stage directions are enclosed in brackets. They describe the characters' moves
- Each character's speech starts on a new line
- The speaker's name is written in capital letters followed by a colon introducing the speech

How to use the paragraph

- There is one occasion on which you must use a paragraph: to separate the spoken words of one character from another:

  'Can you tell me how to get to town from here?'
  'How do you want to go?' I asked. 'By bus?'
  'Yes,' she said.
  'The quickest way or the prettiest way?'
  'Oh, definitely the prettiest,' she smiled.

Notice that you can follow the conversation very easily and you don't need to keep putting in 'he said', 'she said', and so on

Remember: we see writing on the page, and an attractive layout is part of the pleasure of reading.

- Apart from that there is no restriction on the length or purpose of a paragraph. It can be as little as a single word in length or several pages long. But when paragraphs are very long, they tend to dismay the reader. Try flicking through the pages of a book that has no paragraphs; the effect is very off-putting. So vary their lengths and use them to signal developments in the story

Top tips for progress

- **The best writing comes from your own experience**

- **Work out a plan so that your writing will not ramble**

- **As you write, refer back to this plan to stay on course**

- **A strong opening makes your reader sit up**

- **Try to make the closing lines relate to the opening ones**

- **Make sure you have used paragraphs**

Writing to imagine, explore or entertain

NON-FICTION AND THE MEDIA

This is one of the widest areas in the GCSE English course because it covers just about everything in life apart from literature! We are daily exposed to different forms of non-fiction writing and to the mass media. They are truly inescapable: from bus timetables to junk mail, from the advertising billboard on your way to school to *EastEnders* when you take a break in your homework, they are everywhere.

Let's explore what the examiner is looking for in your response to Non-fiction and the Media.

3 Competent

The candidate communicates different ideas clearly to the reader, presenting a wide range of material in a variety of interesting ways.

2 Good

Candidates present material attractively, covering complicated subject matter clearly and in detail. They can understand the way meaning changes according to the way in which an article is laid out and structured.

1 High Level

Candidates' work is carefully tailored to suit the target audience. They are capable of expressing complex ideas, arguments and meanings. They are able to convey their own ideas with confidence and clarity.

Non-fiction writing

Put simply, a non-fiction text is one that is giving information. Throughout your life, you will constantly have to deal with non-fiction in a wide range of situations, of which these are just a few examples:

- Income tax forms
- Television schedules
- Medical advice pamphlets
- Travel brochures
- Timetables
- Junk mail

Are you a winner or is it junk mail?

One morning you receive an interesting looking envelope.

The envelope reads: Private and Confidential – Strictly for person named below.

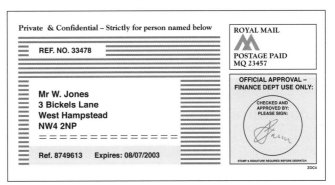

Below the stamp is a box headed: OFFICIAL APPROVAL – FINANCE DEPT USE ONLY. There is a stamp marked CHECKED and APPROVED BY and someone has signed inside that stamp. Smaller capital letters below this state: 'Stamp and signature required before despatch'.

Comment

Before you even get as far as opening this envelope, the signs are that this is an official document, with words like, 'Confidential' and 'Approved by' and 'Finance Dept', adding to the impression that this comes from a government office and demands attention.

Inside you discover writing in a large box that says:

Mr W Jones
Your Special Winners
Receipt Number is: 89081

If your Special Winners Receipt Number matches one of those in the list opposite, then you have definitely been allocated one of the amazing awards below!

Winners can call this number: 0123 456 7890 to find out which award you have been allocated.

MR W JONES Your Special Winners Receipt Number is: **89081** If your Special Winners Receipt Number matches one of those in the list opposite, then you have definitely been allocated one of the amazing awards below! Winners can call this number **0123 456 7890** to find out which award you have been allocated.	**THE OFFICIAL LIST OF SPECIAL WINNERS RECEIPT NUMBERS** Below are the randomly selected winning numbers chosen by our computers. If your pre-allocated Special Winners Receipt Number matches one of those on the list below then you've definitely been allocated one of the amazing awards!

85272	83662	84573
82114	87591	89081
84371	81344	82828

CHECKED AND APPROVED BY: PLEASE SIGN:

Total Selected: 9 (Nine)
KEEP THIS DOCUMENT SAFE

Beside this box is some more writing headed:
THE OFFICIAL LIST OF SPECIAL WINNERS RECEIPT NUMBERS with another seal stamped and approved and a warning *'KEEP THIS DOCUMENT SAFE'*.

Amongst the nine numbers… tucked away where you don't immediately spot it is…Yes! Your number!

A second page has a list entitled: *WINNERS INFORMATION ONLY*, which reveals a range of prizes, including lots of cash, a computer and a Canary Islands 7-night Stay.

All you have to do is send a first class stamp – unattached – or ring the number given.

Comment
It probably will surprise you that you are a winner. What a stroke of luck to get one of the winning numbers. The letter is now a Document, important and certainly genuine…

So are you a winner? Well, what do you think?

The envelope offers just a little extra help. On the back of it there are 22 lines of very tiny writing in block capitals. (TINY BLOCK CAPITALS BY THE WAY ARE HARDER TO READ THAN LOWER CASE LETTERS, don't you agree!) On line 12, you can just make out that among the prizes are 5 x computers and 3000 x holiday accommodation in the Canary Islands.

This is what you will win. But you must pay for the flights and book them through the company that sent you this letter and you can only go on holiday for seven days at dates selected by them in May and June.

This will almost certainly be in a timeshare where you will spend a week being chased by a plausible man trying to persuade you to buy a week of timeshare accommodation.

Final comment
Non-fiction does not mean fact. Whenever someone offers you something for nothing, there is generally the scent of a rat somewhere if you can find it! Remember the following approach:

- **B**e sceptical
- **I**nvestigate who it's from
- **N**otice the wording
- **I**dentify your prize
- **T**hrow it away

If that is too difficult to remember, just remember the initial letters: **BIN IT**!

Non-fiction that is worth reading

Some non-fiction is positively essential reading. Human beings learn from their experiences and pass their knowledge on to the rest of humanity, most commonly by writing it down. One of the key areas where we have to learn from others is health.

Look at the information below on meningitis and septicaemia:

Symptoms of meningitis: severe headache, stiff neck (unusual in children), dislike of bright lights (unusual in children), fever or vomiting, drowsiness or impaired consciousness, a rash

Symptoms of septicaemia: a rash, fever and vomiting, cold hands and feet, rapid breathing, stomach or joint or muscle pain, sometimes with diarrhoea, drowsiness or impaired consciousness

Babies may suffer from: tense or bulging soft spot on their head, blotchy skin (getting paler or turning blue), refusal to feed, irritability when picked up with a high-pitched or moaning cry, stiff body with jerky movements or else floppy and lifeless

The symptoms can appear in any order; not everyone gets all these symptoms; septicaemia can occur with or without meningitis

Remember, trust your instincts. Someone who has meningitis or septicaemia needs medical help urgently. *(Information courtesy of Meningitis Research Foundation)*

This is vital information but the way it is presented here is not very helpful for someone who is desperately worried about the person in their household who might have meningitis. To improve the information:

- Bullet points will help highlight key facts
- Illustrations of the various symptoms focus the mind quickly on what to look for

Try for yourself to see how you can convert the information into a more easily understood form. Think of those pamphlets you pick up at the doctor's and see if you can design a similar one for Meningitis and Septicaemia.

When you have finished, look at the Meningitis Research Foundation website and see how they have solved the problem (www.meningitis.org/symptoms).

Top tips for progress

- **Decide who your target audience is and in what situation they will read this information**

- **Use language that suits the reader**

- **Break up the information into stages**

- **Layout is vital in presenting staged information**

The mass media

The mass media is the name given to the different organisations that communicate to our society. The term covers television and radio, newspapers and magazines, advertising and the internet.

What they have in common is that their communications reach vast numbers of people. They are studied for GCSE because if people we do not know are communicating with us, it helps to understand what they are trying to sell us, so to speak! Be in no doubt at all, they are trying to sell us something!

The other thing that the mass media do is to show us what sort of a society we live in. If they are going to sell us something, they have to be able to identify with us. There is no point in advertising snowmobiles, since we do not live in the Arctic and hardly have much need for them.

Television advertising, for instance, creates little scenes from everyday life in Britain so through the advert we see ourselves. And strangely, the adverts create us too! By picturing ourselves with the advertised product, we write a little story for our own lives.

That is not a cynical statement. We live in a free and wealthy society. We can do what we like within the law and can spend our hard-earned money in any way we choose. What a study of the mass media attempts is to enable you to be discriminating.

Television

This is the biggest of the media. Hardly anyone does not possess or see a television set so it's quite a good starting point. Recent technological developments have seen an enormous expansion in the numbers of programme providers and consequently what is available on television. Where the television companies find their finance determines the nature of what is shown. A very short history might be helpful.

Potted histories

Public Service Broadcasting: the BBC

The British Broadcasting Corporation was set up as a public service in 1922 under John Reith as its General Manager. It was committed to 'educate, inform and entertain' the general public. These remain the BBC's three aims. The order of the words is worth noting since they represent the order of priorities when it comes to spending our money.

Educational broadcasting began on radio in 1926. Though the first TV broadcast was made in 1936, it did not become a national service until the early 1950s. The key date here was 2 June, 1953 – the Coronation of Queen Elizabeth II. An estimated 20 million viewers watched the events in darkened rooms as the rain poured down that day in London. By the end of the 1950s, television coverage extended to 95 per cent of the population.

The 1960s saw the first live broadcast via Telstar from America (1962). England won the 1966 World Cup on the BBC. BBC2 was added in the mid-sixties and by 1967 the first pictures in colour were being screened though no one thought it would last! By 1969, we were able to see live pictures of the first moon landing. In the 1970s the BBC set up the Open University service enabling anyone to take a degree.

In 2012, the BBC now broadcasts in HD (high-definition) and it has launched the iPlayer enabling viewers to watch many of the most popular programmes on their computers and other digital devices.

The BBC remains a public-owned corporation and since it is funded by the money we pay for our television licenses we are entitled to a say in the way it is run.

Independent Television

Initially three television companies served three regions: London, the North and the Midlands. Companies bought the right to provide programmes in their area, though a small percentage of their output had to be based on the region. The original idea has not changed even though there are many more TV companies. Each region still has its own company which generates local news and local programmes.

ITV was launched on 22 September, 1955, the same day as Grace Archer died in a fire on BBC's popular radio serial, *The Archers*. This tells you something of the nature of the relationship between the two main television services in Britain.

A look at the first night's schedule gives some idea of how ITV felt it would compete with the BBC monopoly:

7.30	The Halle Orchestra playing classical music	10.00	News and Newsreel
7.45	Speeches from public figures	10.15	Gala Night at the Mayfair
8.00	A Variety show	10.30	Star Cabaret
8.40	Three play excerpts	10.50	Preview: programme trailers
9.10	Professional Boxing	11.00	Epilogue
			The National Anthem and close-down

This glittering evening had over half the nation as its audience despite Grace Archer's death!

ITV gained an extra channel in 1982 so that it could continue to compete with the BBC, and further channels have been added in recent years.

It is funded mainly by the advertisements it screens and in order to be able to earn this money, it has to attract as big an audience as possible. The relationship between the mass media and the advertising industry explains a great deal about the nature of the programmes we see on ITV.

Programmes are scheduled according to the sort of people who may be watching at a particular time of day.

NON-FICTION AND THE MEDIA

Satellite and cable television

Improvements in communications have led to a massive increase in the number of television programmes that are available. Television signals are bounced off satellites or fed down telephone cables and can span the world at the speed of light. In 1962, the first black and white live pictures of America were shown on television. Today we have scores of programmes in colour coming simultaneously from the furthest points of the earth.

All of them depend on revenue from advertising even though subscribers are obliged to pay either monthly subscriptions or one-off fees for special events.

We now have a vast range of different options twenty-four hours a day, literally adding up to hundreds of choices. The choices are so vast, it is impossible to provide a complete coverage in this book so we shall look only at a few of the most popular programmes and show you how to prepare a media response.

Television genres

'Genre' is the word used to describe a type of literature or television programme.

Soaps

The term 'soap opera' was originally applied to American radio serials that were paid for by soap companies. *Chambers Dictionary* defines a soap opera as:

'a sentimental, melodramatic serial…written around the lives of the members of a family or other small group, and chiefly concerned with the emotional involvement of the characters'.

Three aspects of that definition require a little more clarification:

● *Sentimental* means a deliberate working up of feelings. In other words, the storyline concentrates on people's emotional responses to issues, often showing them in a way that is not natural. In a soap a character might feel very upset about the way another character is behaving. In real life, this rarely ends up in a violent argument. Generally speaking, if we are upset, we tend to say nothing. This would not make very good television!

● *Melodramatic* is used to describe a play that is romantic and sensational. People get what they deserve and a happy ending is vital. A bit like a pantomime. Once again, real life is not like that. People rarely get what they deserve. In fact, what happens is frequently the opposite of that: nice people end up unhappy and nasty people often profit from their nastiness! If a soap ignored people's unpleasant behaviour, we might think that it was unrealistic and unbelievable. Life isn't neat and everything doesn't always balance out

● *Emotional involvement*
describes the way characters' feelings are influenced by others. The stronger their feelings the better of course, because it makes good television

The very fact that there are so many soaps shows how important they are to the viewing public. Make a list of the ones you like in their order of appeal and ask a friend to do the same. The comparison might show you that both of you being of a similar age and outlook enjoy the same things. Now do the same with a parent, and then again with a grandparent. Now you will see that the lists begin to look very different.

This will give you a rough idea of the target audience of the various soaps.

On commercial channels there is another way of discovering this – without ever actually watching the programmes at all! How could this be done? Well, the answer lies in the advertisements.

Take the Christmas episode of *Coronation Street* in December 2011, which attracted a huge audience of 9.9 million people. If you have a huge audience you can sell advertising space very expensively.

During this 45-minute episode – sponsored by a furniture chain – there were nine advertisements. These were for:

1. A children's cereal
2. A skincare product promising perfect skin
3. An advert about mental health
4. A dance fitness game
5. A fast-food chain advertising their coffee
6. A hair shampoo promising stronger hair
7. A low-calorie savoury biscuit
8. A car with extra safety features
9. A mucus relief advert

Soaps are shown in the early evening since they are regarded as family entertainment.

Without being too much of a genius, you might reasonably conclude that the sort of people who were watching were families on uncomfortable sofas, with tired skin and brittle hair, bunged up with mucus, hoping to get back into shape after the excesses of Christmas, worried about their car in the winter weather and even more worried about Uncle Stan who didn't come this Christmas because he suffers from depression and maybe they should invite him for a coffee and a chat in the New Year.

Advertisers are always trying to sell something: be sceptical.

That may be a bit over the top but who else would buy those products and presumably watch that sort of programme?

The BBC does not offer such handy short cuts to identifying target audiences but there are one or two subtle pointers you can use. Their flagship soap – *EastEnders* – is scheduled at very much the same time as *Coronation Street* but never at the same time. If it was appealing to a different audience, they could screen it at the same time. The truth of the matter is that both soaps are appealing to the same audience.

Emmerdale is another programme broadcast several times a week. It occupies a key slot in an evening's schedules at 7.00 p.m. People have just finished their evening meal and are settling down to a night's viewing. What better time to grab their attention, especially since most will continue to watch that television channel for the rest of the evening.

In 2002 the television schedulers added another little trick to their act – by telling viewers as the programme is ending what is coming next, to encourage them not to change channel!

If you are asked to review an episode of a soap, look out for the following devices which are used to engage the viewers' interest:

- Characters 'overhearing' information that is private

- Characters having to tell a person something they think he or she ought to know

- Characters misunderstanding something important and acting as if it is true

- Similar storylines in the same episode

- Characters determined to make up for mistakes

- People falling for each other's partners

- Cliffhangers at the end of an episode to encourage you to watch the next episode

These are just a few things to look out for. See if you can add to the list with your own observations.

One final point worth noting about soaps is that they frequently tackle difficult social issues or issues of public importance:

- Child abuse
- Domestic violence
- Gay relationships
- Divorce
- Drug taking

These programmes provide a public service in this respect since they keep the viewer aware of social problems and their possible solutions. More significantly, they help to influence public opinion by the way they handle social problems.

One character in *Coronation Street*, Hayley, turned out to have had an interesting past which necessitated her having a sex-change operation. She was drawn as a sympathetic character, all sweet and giggling and helpful, so that when nasty comments were made about her, we sprang to her defence along with the goodies in the *Coronation Street* cast. Thus a difficult subject was tackled and we were led to believe that, in a normal society, people with such backgrounds were only disliked by the intolerant bully.

NON-FICTION AND THE MEDIA

Reality television and docu-soaps

One of people's commonest characteristics is nosiness! It can be a positive thing: if we are interested in the way others behave, we may learn lessons for ourselves, and we can also see where our help is needed. The blunt truth is that we are fascinated by the way other people live their lives.

The first example of reality television was a fly-on-the-wall documentary about a family in Reading, entitled simply *The Family* (1974). It was a series of programmes, made by Paul Watson, following the lives of a very ordinary family. It showed everything: family arguments, loves and illnesses, problems and rows. This was such an important milestone in television history that it was awarded its very own name – a docu-soap, or factual everyday drama.

A host of similar programmes followed showing daily activity in all walks of life: in airports, shops, hotels, cruise liners, schools, hospitals, veterinary practices, doctors' surgeries, police stations…anywhere in fact that anyone works!

Then, along came *Big Brother* in 2000. Ordinary people are shut up in a studio watched round the clock by cameras, and one by one they are voted out. The last one wins the big prize though by that time all the contestants have become national figures and, win or lose, gain what they all want: celebrity status. It has been so successful that *Big Brother* has been adapted for TV audiences around the world.

There is a strong element of manipulation by the programme makers. Television cannot afford to be boring so the contestants are carefully selected to ensure that, at the very least, there will be friction. The programme makers are no less interested in sexual chemistry, though there seem to be a lot more rows than love affairs.

Examiner's Tip
Always read the entire exam paper before you begin planning your answers.

Celebrity television

Following the success of reality TV, someone had the bright idea of using ready-made celebrities – or to be more accurate, glamorous newcomers and ageing failures who desperately craved the limelight. An early contender in 'Help A Celebrity' was *Celebrity Big Brother* but the ideas grew ever more ingenious with celebrities (some of them, it has to be said, virtually unknown!) stranded in the jungle in *I'm a Celebrity Get Me Out of Here!* and learning to dance in *Strictly Come Dancing*.

Celebrities are also conscripted to appear in quiz shows such as *Celebrity Who Wants to Be a Millionaire* and *Million Pound Drop*. The difference here is that whatever they win is donated to their nominated charity. So what's in it for them? Well, it is great PR! They can show off their intelligence, whilst giving the impression that they are very nice people willing to give their time to help the needy. Being on prime-time TV can only do their careers some good, even if they don't get many of the questions right!

The watershed

This is another word for the point in the evening after which programme makers can screen material that is better suited to adult viewing rather than general family viewing. In Britain this happens at 9.00 p.m. when it is assumed that children are safely tucked up in bed!

Radio

Radio is still a very popular medium in the UK although the way we listen has changed. Many of us now listen on MP3 players, computers, TVs and phones rather than single receivers and stereos.

The principal radio broadcaster is the BBC which now has a vast range of stations from national networked stations like Radios 1 to 5, digital organisations and a country-wide wall of local radio stations. On top of British domestic services, the BBC runs the World Service which reaches across the globe 24-hours a day, bringing the news and features programmes. BBC radio is free though it raises its revenue from the television licence fee that we all pay. There are also many independent radio stations whose money comes from advertising.

NON-FICTION
AND THE MEDIA

THE ARCHERS
ON AIR

Radio soaps

The original soap operas were on US radio but in Britain we have our own long-running serial – *The Archers* – which has been on air since 1950 and celebrated its 60th anniversary in January 2011, clocking up over 16,300 episodes.

It started as an educational programme for farmers showing them how best to feed a population that was still subject to post-war rationing. It became a general entertainment programme in 1972 and regularly attracts large audiences. In 2011, it was reported to have an average weekly reach of over 5 million listeners!

Radio dramas

It may seem obvious but radio only appeals to the single sense of hearing. For that reason it develops the listener's imagination. A little boy was asked whether he preferred television or radio and answered that radio was his favourite because 'the scenery is better'. This may or may not be true but you can see what he was trying to say, that it engaged his imagination and he was able to create his own wonderful scenery.

Sound effects are crucial and you can have great fun investigating how to create a scene simply through sound. It makes a very good subject for a Speaking and Listening assignment.

Another possible assignment for Speaking and Listening is devising a commentary on a sporting event, for example. You may discover that you have a talent for it and if you have, you can offer your services to hospital radio or even try to get a job with the big boys in the BBC or independent radio!

Advertising

Advertising is one of the main sources of revenue in all aspects of the mass media so the opportunities for analysis are plentiful. All advertising in Britain is controlled by the Advertising Standards Authority (ASA) and its principles are used to judge the correctness of any advertisement:

- All advertisements should be legal, decent, honest and truthful
- All advertisements should be prepared with a sense of responsibility to consumers and to society
- No advertisement should bring advertising into disrepute

If you feel that an advertisement does not conform to any of the above, you are entitled to complain to the ASA.

Analysis of an advertisement

There are so many products advertised, it is difficult to supply a single right way of studying any advert.

The sort of things you need to bear in mind are:

- Where the advertisement is displayed – products are targeted at different consumers so advertisers will select the appropriate place
- The message of the advert – how it is attempting to sell the product
- The wording of the advert and how it suits the medium in which it appears
- The pictures used and how they reinforce the message the advertiser wishes to convey
- How successful you think it is

Look at this advertisement which appeared on the back cover of a theatre programme.

The advertiser is linking his product with the likely reader. We are in a theatre so we can be expected to find a reference to theatre and might even smile at the wording. Having a sympathetic reader is crucial to the success of an advert.

The wording – or copy, as it is known in the trade – is:

**Here's the cast.
Imagine the performance.**

Ranged around the page are four small pictures of various Volkswagen cars, in reds and blues, with a larger picture of a blue Golf GTI. In the lower third of the panel, there is the familiar VW logo and centrally placed at the bottom of the advert is the name of the local dealer with details of address and website.

The cars are pictured from different angles so that the eye moves around the page looking at each of them and noting the difference in models. Using red and blue car models makes them stand out on the page.

These are expensive cars but you could reasonably expect the people who attended the theatre to be quite well paid and so able to afford them. The cleverness of the advert's wording and the simplicity of the layout made this quite an attractive advert and therefore quite likely to be successful.

Television advertising

The entire content of television programmes, including advertising, is regulated by the Independent Television Commission (ITC) and what may be shown is strictly controlled by them.

The sort of assignment you are likely to be set might be an analysis of an advert or series of adverts for a product.

Follow a pattern of this sort:

1. Name the product and the time and date of the advertisement.
2. Describe the nature of the advert.
3. Identify what in your view makes the product desirable.
4. Identify and explain your view of the likely target of the advert: i.e. age, sex and status.
5. Show how you think the advertiser is attempting to sell the product.
6. Evaluate the success of the advertisement.

A typical response might look something like this:

Double Cheez Dippers: 14th January, 15:45

A woolly-toy type black sheep comes across a field towards the camera. She does a rap telling the viewer about her enjoyment in eating Double Cheez Dippers. We are shown a close-up of a breadstick being dipped first into a cheese spread, then into 'delicious bacon bits'.

The notion of a black sheep enjoying this sort of dip is an amusing one and would appeal to young children.

A mother sitting with the child would find the sheep appealing and the snack itself seems tasty. Dipping a breadstick is as easy for a young child with little fingers as it is for a sheep with hooves, and being outside gets across the idea that the product would be ideal for picnics and packed lunches.

The advert is concentrating on the concept that this is a fun food, cheap and easy to consume.

It seems quite a successful advert. The central character is a black sheep who we expect to be a little daring. The supermarket chains would have been made aware of the TV advertising campaign so they can stock up in advance.

AOL: 14th January, 15:47

A rapid succession of moving pictures cross the screen. A variety of voices tell us of the advantages of using this Internet Service Provider: 'good for homework…good for online shopping…tells you about stocks and shares…free sport…entertainment'.

Two million people are claimed to use the service so when you join AOL, you belong to an organisation that many others have found advantageous. The various aspects that have been highlighted tell of a service that is serious and worth having, perhaps particularly for mothers and children.

The appeal is a simple one: look, lots of people use us. We offer free trials – what have you got to lose!

It is hard to see why this should not be a successful advert. It may not actually sell a single thing to the viewer this afternoon but it helps to establish the brand name as being reliable.

It is hard to justify having any advertisements during a children's TV programme and in fact there were only two adverts in this space, which suggests that it is not a very commercially attractive time or place to advertise. It is likely that there will be only two types of viewer: young children (who do not have money to spend) and mothers (who have plenty of other things to spend their money on!).

We might well conclude that the advertiser is hoping that the child will badger his/her mother into buying Cheez Dippers, and that AOL are offering Mum the promise of being able to enjoy herself on the internet when her child is safely tucked up in bed.

Non-fiction and the Media

Britain's geographical location and the density of our population means that have always enjoyed a vigorous daily newspaper industry, although circulation numbers are declining because of the internet. Newspapers used to be divided into two categories: broadsheet and tabloid. The terms describe the size of the newspaper – tabloids were half the size of broadsheets – but some broadsheets are now tabloid size.

There is a variety of other newspaper productions such as local newspapers, free newspapers and evening papers. Each of the publications has its own target readership and style.

Tabloids (aka Red Tops)

The main publications are *The Sun, Daily Mirror, Daily Mail, Daily Express* and *Daily Star*. They are easy to read and tend to sensationalise the news. The lack of depth means that their journalists concentrate on quite a narrow view.

Broadsheets (aka the Quality Press)

These are altogether heavier not only in terms of actual weight but also in the way they handle news stories. Four newspapers come into this category: *The Times, The Independent, The Guardian* and *The Daily Telegraph*. They aim to present a balanced view of subjects with abundant background information that will enable the reader to form his own balanced judgement of what is happening in the world.

Local newspapers

As their name suggests, these publications rarely stray beyond their own neighbourhood to consider national stories. They usually appear weekly and tell communities about themselves. They enable readers to know what is happening locally, naming and shaming local villains and commending the works of local heroes. The local newspaper businesses have shrunk in recent years and most communities rely on a single newspaper. This can be a problem since if you disagree with the local rag's coverage of a story there is no one to complain to!

Evening newspapers

Few areas of the country are able to support evening newspapers so they are restricted to the larger cities such as London, Manchester and Birmingham. They carry national news along with important local stories, sporting fixtures and local advertisements for entertainment and house sales, for instance.

Free newspapers

There has been a sharp rise in the number of free papers in recent years – these rely solely upon advertising for their revenue. As they are distributed free, advertisers know the circulation will be high but there is less non-advertising content for readers.

Analysis of a newspaper story

Task: *Compare the treatment of the same story in different newspapers*

You might structure your response in this way:

1. Identify the nature of the two newspapers you have selected. For convenience, it is wise to choose a story that appears in both a tabloid and broadsheet, so explain the difference between these.
2. Observe the different layout of the story: the headlines, the use of photographs.
3. Consider the ways in which the language varies.
4. Offer your thoughts on the way the story comes across: whether a particular aspect is stressed in one paper for example, and attempt to explain this.
5. Conclude with a personal opinion on the merits and disadvantages of each, supporting your opinions with examples taken from the newspapers.

A study of national newspapers in October 2011

Ten national newspapers were available. Their prices and average circulation figures were:

The Sun 30p (2,715,473)
Daily Mirror 45p (1,118,120)
Daily Star 30p (658,690)
Daily Express 45p (614,534)
Daily Mail 55p (1,998,363)
The Times £1.00 (417,197)
The Guardian £1.20 (230,541)
The Independent £1.00 (133,449)
The Daily Telegraph £1.00 (603,901)
i 20p (211,467)
(Source of figures: *ABC*)

Comment

The prices are interesting since they tell you who is competing against whom.

The Sun *and the* Daily Mirror *are in direct competition, as are the* Daily Express *and* Daily Mail, *who are a bit more serious in tone than the other tabloids. The* Daily Express *and the* Daily Mirror *keep their price lower probably in the hope of attracting some of their competitors' many readers.*

Of the broadsheets The Guardian *is the most expensive. The move to raise its price was risky, but while it did lose some readers, most stayed loyal so the paper's revenue actually increased.* The Daily Telegraph *was soon to follow their lead in November 2011.*

The newest paper is i, *launched in 2010 by the publishers of* The Independent. *It is aimed at readers 'with little time but wanting a quality paper'. At 20p it undercuts them all.*

NON-FICTION
AND THE MEDIA

The main story

Here are the front covers of newspapers on 15th January 2003, the day when the big news was the death of a policeman in Manchester during a raid on a flat whose inhabitants were suspected of some kind of terrorist involvement. In the wider world, there was the threat of war with Iraq.

Comment

The word used to describe the victim is interesting. 'Cop' and 'copper' are both slang words though perhaps a 'cop' is a more menacing character than the affectionate 'copper'! The Daily Mail *uses a grander word while the quality papers all plump for the neutral, 'policeman'.*

The assault itself is described in different terms: 'Copper knifed to death' is the most dramatic. Four of the papers attempt a link between this and a recent story about terrorists being arrested in London for possession of the poison ricin, which could be used for terrorist purposes. They use ricin as an adjective to describe a raid or a suspect.

Only six of the papers treat the murder as the main story. The Daily Star *seems to confuse soap opera and reality – two bloodbaths in one week, and the real one is on Page 2! It is interesting that the then Editor of the* Daily Star, *Peter Hill, claimed he had a simple strategy for success (and the* Daily Star's *circulation was growing): 'If it's on TV, it's in the* Daily Star'. *He believed that crime stories do not sell newspapers nor do stories about ordinary people, because 'ordinary people do not want to read about each other'!*

The Guardian *and* The Independent *both have political stories – a proposed English cricket match against Zimbabwe, and the continuing worries about war with Iraq, which resulted in the US invasion only two months later.*

Photographs

The Sun	has a small picture of blue-coated policemen looking at the front windows of a house, 'Raid…cops in Manchester last night'.
Daily Mirror	has a small picture of 'The forensic team at scene last night', showing a policeman in a grey plastic suit walking between several wheelie bins.
Daily Star	has a large picture of Chardonnay, a television footballer's wife, whose ample bosom is barely concealed, plus a smaller picture of the *Coronation Street* murderer.
Daily Express	has two pictures, a large one of a police car and van, and a larger photo of the same policeman as in the *The Sun*. 'COVER-UP: an officer at the death scene'.
Daily Mail	has a large picture of four policemen dressed in blue overalls standing in front of a house.
The Times	has a large picture of the Queen and a map of the Manchester area showing where the murder happened.
The Guardian	has a picture of anti-war protesters holding a banner in front of a ship.
The Independent	has a large photo of an art exhibit, 'a Diana voodoo doll'.
The Daily Telegraph	has the same picture as the *Daily Mail* (slightly altered) showing the police search of the garden, plus a small picture of Manchester's assistant Chief Constable, 'last night'.

Comment

You wouldn't expect very graphic pictures so early in a murder enquiry. The photographers are kept at a distance by the police so they have limited photo opportunities. The fact that the same photo appears twice suggests that newspapers buy them in from agencies who send photographers to cover events. The choice of a policeman by a dustbin conveys the impression of a sleazy, sordid area. The one of the house with police in the garden is a rather sinister picture. The Daily Star *is obviously keen to satisfy its male readers!*

Non-fiction and the Media

The opening sentence

News stories are generally summed up in the first sentence. The shorter the better for the tabloids!

The Sun:
'A hero detective was stabbed to death yesterday as police raided a suspected terror cell involved in the ricin poison plot'.

Daily Mirror:
'A policeman was stabbed to death through the chest with a kitchen knife as officers swooped on suspected ricin terrorists last night'.

Daily Star:
'Tricky Dicky Hillman's bloody rampage helped Coronation Street give its BBC rival a battering at last'.

Daily Express:
'A policeman was killed and four other officers were injured last night when they were attacked by a gang of suspected Al Qaeda terrorists'.

Daily Mail:
'A Special Branch detective was stabbed to death by a suspected Al Qaeda terrorist last night'.

The Times:
'A police officer was stabbed to death and another was seriously injured when police raided a flat in north Manchester last night as part of the investigation into the discovery of the poison ricin'.

The Guardian:
'A police officer was stabbed to death and five others were injured last night during an anti-terrorist operation linked to the discovery last week of the lethal poison ricin'.

The Independent:
'A policeman died after he was stabbed in the chest during an anti-terrorist operation in Manchester yesterday that was linked to the discovery of ricin poison in London'.

The Daily Telegraph:
'A policeman was stabbed to death and four others injured last night as they tried to arrest a man wanted after a tip-off about the production of the deadly poison ricin'.

Comment

The Sun *and the* Daily Mirror *focus on sensational details, 'a hero detective…raided a suspected terror cell'. The* Daily Express *is straight to the point whilst the* Daily Mail *manages to sum up the story in sixteen words. The* Daily Star *uses the same number of words with the important difference that the murder was a fictional one!*

All four broadsheets use a longer opening sentence. There is a little confusion as to how many were injured, any number from one to five. The language is slightly more difficult in them too: 'anti-terrorist operations' are referred to and ricin is described as 'lethal' rather than 'deadly'. The language used suggests that each paper's readership has different reading abilities which in turn suggests that they may have different interests and spending priorities.

Closing thoughts about the papers on 15th January 2003

This news story was in its early stages. It happened late in the evening before the papers were published and the reporters would have had three sources: official police reports, unofficial police contacts and casual witnesses. The murder of a police officer is always a grave matter: his or her job is to protect our society from lawlessness so the death of an officer is more shocking than that of a private individual. The murder of a person charged with enforcing the law shows how dangerous their enemies are, for all of us.

What's in a name?

Do you think a newspaper's name matters? The Daily Mirror *offers a reflection of day-to-day life.* The Sun *rises bright and early and livens us all up. The* Daily Star *twinkles like Venus in the morning sky. The* Daily Express *rushes us the news. The* Daily Mail *comes daily like the post.* The Daily Telegraph *is an old-fashioned means of communication.* The Independent *informs us gravely that it makes up its own mind.* The Guardian *is a kindly uncle looking after us while* The Times *covers everything!*

The police officer concerned would have family, friends and colleagues who would be deeply distressed so there is a real need for journalists to be sensitive and not to intrude on private grief.

Since the full story was not yet known, it was dangerous to jump to conclusions but, as it turned out, these initial reports were accurate. An al-Queda suspect, Kamel Bourgass, was jailed in 2004 for the murder of Detective Constable Stephen Oake. Three other police officers were injured in the attack.

NON-FICTION
AND THE MEDIA

News as treated on television, radio and in the newspapers

The essential difference is that television reporters are able to broadcast up-to-the-minute accounts of what is happening. Thus we can see the story breaking and developing. A newspaper has an early morning deadline and has to form an opinion that will be on breakfast tables.

Television news stories rely on pictures and interviews, whilst newspapers use photos from agencies and words. If there are no pictures, there is no TV news. Very often, having the pictures enables television news programmes to make their own news. Think of the dramatic news coverage of things that happen far away and have absolutely no bearing on life in Britain: a hurricane in the Pacific, a single-seater plane crash viewed as it happened, a terrible mudslide.

Real news or not?

Television's reliance upon pictures means that occasionally it can manufacture its own news. This can happen when a news programme has dramatic footage or wants to plug another programme on their channel.

An example of this occurred on Monday 20th January, 2003, at a time when the build-up to a possible war was dominating the media. The main story on the ITN early evening news concerned a man who had travelled that day with his wife to a clinic in Switzerland. He was suffering from a terminal disease and had decided to end his life.

This was hardly world-shattering news and was not even touched upon in the competing BBC news. The reason for the prominence given to the story rapidly became clear. Trevor McDonald's news magazine was running a feature on this story an hour or so later, making the news itself a sort of trailer for his programme.

Radio relies on the spoken word and sound effects. Listeners use their imaginations to visualise what is going on. A news report has to be very clear since we do not have the freedom to read it over again as we do in a paper. It is very good at bringing us eye-witness reports.

Examiner's Tip
An hour-long examination essay is about 500 words in length.

Magazines

In Britain we benefit from a wide array of magazines. They have a clearly identified target readership, covering all ages, both sexes, interests, hobbies, pastimes, sports and tastes.

Conduct a survey of the students in your class and build up a top ten of magazines. Repeat this survey with other students in your school or college and you will be able to form some idea of the range of publications that cater for the youth market.

A typical young people's magazine will cover:

- Style
- Friends
- The opposite sex
- Education
- Careers
- The stars
- Fashion
- Fitness
- Problem pages
- Music
- Quizzes

heat: 14th January 2012

One of the most popular magazines is *heat* and a brief look at the contents of one issue will give an interesting snapshot of what it considers to be important to its readers.

On the front cover, the big news was about the breakdown of a celebrity marriage; the revelation that a member of a girl group has an addiction problem; and the supposed 'scandal' of a boy band member tweeting a rather revealing picture of himself on Twitter.

Inside there is more news.

A famous pop singer has a new boyfriend and she is totally smitten.

The answer to the big question: why the king of the talent shows wants a judge of a rival TV programme to join his show.

Elsewhere there is an interview with the actors who play two 'hot' *Eastenders* brothers over a game of poker; an analysis of a Hollywood actor's taste in women; and why a photo of her ex with another woman drove one celebrity model mad. We learn that 'even paper pants leave a mark' when a famous fashion model is photographed in a skimpy bodysuit with the

tell-tale fake tan lines. There are pictures of the aforementioned king of the talent shows on the yacht he chartered for £285,000 a week; a few celebrity couples in beach 'pda' alerts; and top tips on wearing faux fur.

There are reviews of films, videos and DVDs, along with the television schedules for the following week.

There are the customary horoscopes that link your future to those of 'The Stars', and *heat* makes the link with celebrity that it feels is vital for its readers: 'At present, you (Aquarians) and Amanda Holden are being forced to stay put. While remaining inert doesn't sit well with water bearers, you could use this time to fine-tune future plans'. Does this mean studying hard for GCSEs?

The advertisements

As with ITV, it is possible to determine who *heat* feels are its readers by looking briefly at the products it advertises. Advertising works because it offers us what we desire, by playing on our fears. It succeeds by offering the lifestyle that we wish to have. By studying adverts we learn about the society in which we live.

This edition of *heat* offered adverts for:

- McCain HomeChips
- London Fashion Week sponsored by Vodafone
- The new foam sensation foundation from Maybelline
- Aussie's Miracle Moist Conditioner
- Fairy dishwasher tablets
- A low-calorie wine
- McDonald's coffee
- Boots No7 Beautiful Skin cream
- The 10 Minute Solution workout DVD
- Driving lessons with BSM
- And a 50% off spray tan offer for every reader!

See if you can work out from this information a profile of the typical *heat* reader.

A media coursework assignment

Make your own magazine. A reasonable sized assignment might consist of:

- A title and front cover
- A feature on music, sport, fashion or beauty
- A problem page (get your friends to supply you with real questions!)
- Sports news or showbiz gossip
- The stars, i.e. horoscopes
- An editorial: your magazine speaks out on a controversial subject

Of course, if you have a brilliant idea, you could try selling it to a publisher!

Films

Film is another of the mass media. It went through the doldrums in the last part of the twentieth century but it made a big comeback with the development of large film complexes that have a dozen or more films showing simultaneously.

Writing about film

One of the suggested assignments for film offered by AQA is 'A comparison of the techniques used in the opening sequence of two films'.

Films are all about stories. Read this and see what is missing:

'A couple are driving fast in a car. They enter a darkened building. A woman is dead.'

Comment

We have difficulty in understanding that this is a story because we cannot understand the causes of what is happening, the identities of the people and the building or the death.

Now look at another description of the same events:

'A telephone call to the couple informs them that one of their mothers is critically ill. They drive fast through the night to be with her. They arrive very late and much of the hospital is in darkness. They make their way to the ward where they find the mother has died.'

Comment
Now it all makes sense and it does so because we understand who the people are, the timescale of the events and the nature of the setting.

When you analyse the opening of a film, you need to identify:

- The characters
- The time
- The setting
- Why they are behaving as they do

If we look at the opening of Alfred Hitchcock's *North by Northwest (1959)*, we know we are in New York in the rush hour: skyscrapers, heavy traffic and pedestrians establish it for us. We see a man leaving a lift with his secretary and walking out of a building, dictating notes. Now we start to pull together ideas. We presume the man is busy and has just come from his office so we get the feeling that we have come in at the middle of a series of events. The film-maker is making us work without our realising it! Since this happens at the beginning of the film we have also seen the credits which are displayed to the accompaniment of music.

The music or sound in the opening credits is helping to establish a mood for us. The actual credits themselves may be presented in a way that is intended to prepare us for what we are about to watch.

Otto Preminger's *The Anatomy of a Murder (1959)* starts with wild jazz music and the credits appear in bits and pieces, very much like the parts of an anatomy.

Oh Brother, Where Art Thou (2001) by the Cohen brothers begins with a spiritual and the sound of metal beaten against metal. The scene gradually clears to reveal prisoners working on a chain gang somewhere in the American Deep South. We are already prisoners ourselves in this appalling heat and we identify with three of them who, as we watch, suddenly detach themselves from the other prisoners and make a break for it.

The study of film can reach very advanced levels so it is helpful in GCSE to work from a very simple theory and see how it relates to your film.

The beginning of a story starts in a state of balance. This balance is upset by something that sets in motion a whole series of other events. Gradually the story moves back towards the balance we had at the beginning, only it is different now.

In the story of the couple driving to an ailing mother, the event that set things in motion was the telephone call. In *Oh Brother, Where Art Thou*, the event was the three men escaping from the chain gang.

In *The Full Monty (1997)* we see a depressed city – Sheffield – and out-of-work men struggling to make ends meet. The film actually starts with a black and white promotional film about Sheffield shot 25 years before the date of this story, which tells us that the steel industry had once provided men with work. The next shot shows two men and a boy looking around a derelict factory for rusty girders to sell. They need to make money and get themselves out of the mess they are in. How will they achieve this? They could strip old factories for cash or they could strip themselves…

In your analysis of the opening of your chosen films, this approach may offer a simple structure:

- Describe any information in the credits that suggests what you are about to see: the background music or sound effects, the credits themselves
- Describe the first scene
- Does the film offer a printed time and date at this point? If so, what is it? If not, where and when do you think the story is set?
- Is there some printed narrative you have to read? If so, why?
- Describe the first places and faces you see
- Describe what the people are doing
- Write what, as far as you can tell, has just happened
- Show how the balance is destroyed
- Describe how the film's end restores the balance
- Show what the events in the film have changed
- Show how your chosen films differ and express a preference if you have one

If you are comparing two films, show how the choices of the film-makers differ. It is easier to cover the films separately but make comparisons since that is the object of the exercise.

Top tips for progress

- **Concentrate your media studies on a narrow range**
- **Always identify the target audience**
- **Consider how layout affects the reader**
- **Have fun. Don't be afraid to employ humour!**

POETRY

GCSE examiners are agreed that of all aspects of the study of English, candidates find most difficulty with poetry. They often go further and observe that most candidates produce work that is below the standard of their other English tasks. So if you can improve your work here, you will certainly do far better in GCSE English than you might have expected.

What is a poem?

The best place, as ever, to start is with a dictionary and find the definition:

'Poem, (noun): a composition in verse; a composition of high beauty of thought or language and artistic form, typically in verse.'

> *Verse*

A poem is written in verse. There is a wide range of verse forms but for GCSE you need only consider the commonest ones.

Blank verse

This is the form used by Shakespeare. It consists of a line of poetry with ten syllables, five of which are stressed, thus giving it a rhythm. This verse form is the nearest we get to the rhythm of normal speech and Shakespeare employs it very cleverly to allow the speaker to sound as if he or she is speaking quite naturally.

'So may the outward shows be least themselves:
The world is still deceived with ornament.'

(*The Merchant of Venice*, Act III Scene ii Lines 73–4)

Rhyming couplets (aka Heroic couplets, Heroic verse)

This is identical to blank verse with the important difference that the lines rhyme in pairs. This verse form has been used from Chaucer in the fourteenth century right up to the present day.

'I know a bank whereon the wild thyme blows,
Where oxlips and the nodding violet grows.'

(*A Midsummer Night's Dream*, II ii 190–191)

The Ballad

This has a four-line stanza (sometimes called a verse itself). The rhyming scheme is most commonly that used by Hood below. It is best used in story-telling since it is light and flows easily.

'Ben Battle was a soldier bold
And used to war's alarms:
But a cannonball took off his legs
So he laid down his arms.'

(*Faithless Nelly Gray*, Thomas Hood)

The rhyming scheme can be varied and provide some amusement:

'Billy, in one of his nice new sashes,
Fell in the fire and was burnt to ashes;
Now, although the room grows chilly,
I haven't the heart to poke poor Billy.'

(*Ruthless Rhymes*, Harry Graham)

The Sonnet

The sonnet is a complicated and short poetic form. It has fourteen lines and a strict rhyming scheme. It was invented by the Italian poet Petrarch for love poetry and has retained its romantic associations. Shakespeare wrote a large number of sonnets and devised his own rhyme, and in the nineteenth century, Wordsworth also devised his own rhyming scheme, and even went so far as to compose a sonnet in its honour!

'Scorn not the Sonnet; Critic, you have frown'd,
Mindless of its just honours; with this key
Shakespeare unlock'd his heart; the melody
Of this small lute gave ease to Petrarch's wound;
A thousand times this pipe did Tasso sound;
With it Camoens sooth'd an exile's grief;
The Sonnet glitter'd a gay myrtle leaf
Amid the cypress with which Dante crown'd
His visionary brow: a glow-worm lamp,
It cheer'd mild Spenser, call'd from Faery-land
To struggle through dark ways; and when a damp
Fell round the path of Milton, in his hand
The Thing became a trumpet; whence he blew
Soul-animating strains – alas, too few!'

(*The Sonnet (ii)*, William Wordsworth)

Examiner's Tip
The high-level candidate can analyse a writer's technique.

He picks out the greatest sonneteers here: Petrarch, Dante and Tasso were Italians; Camoens was Portuguese and exiled to Goa for an unwise love affair; Edmund Spenser and John Milton were English writers, Spenser best known for his poem *The Faery Queen* (Elizabeth I) and Milton (who ultimately went blind) for *Paradise Lost*. The sonnet is portrayed as different sorts of musical instruments. Wordsworth very modestly does not include his name amongst the greats. Perhaps he ran out of lines!

The Haiku

This is a Japanese verse form. It has seventeen syllables arranged in three lines: Line 1 has five syllables, Line 2 has seven and Line 3 has five. The two examples below show different ways of saying the same thing!

'First autumn morning:
the mirror I stare into
shows my father's face.'

(Kijo Murakami)

'The leaves have fallen
And the snow has fallen too
Soon my hair also…'

(Wendy Cope)

Free verse

Most poetry does not attempt to conform to any particular pattern and the poet uses rhythm and rhyme freely to express feelings and ideas.

Poetic language

If you look at the examples of poetry shown above, you will notice that the language is very varied. In fact, it is impossible to describe it in a single line. What all poetic language has in common is that:

- Each word is chosen with great exactness
- No word is wasted
- Expression is original and rhythmic

The poet has chosen his words with extreme care. No word is used accidentally so we need to work out why he has used these exact words.

People often accuse English students of reading too much into a poem. The very best way to find out what a poet is saying is to listen to the poem being read by the person who wrote it. If you cannot do that, then try to hear it spoken by a professional actor.

Plays are meant to be seen on a stage. Poems are meant to be listened to.

There is an additional reason for listening to poetry: the rhythm, rhyme and vocabulary all have a sound, almost a music of words. If you were a brilliant musician you might enjoy reading the score of a piece of music, but you know you are better off hearing it. The same is true for poetry.

Alliteration

This is when a writer repeats the same letter sound for effect – it won't happen accidentally.

You can see it in a tongue-twister like, *'Round the rugged rock the ragged rascal ran'* and in a proper piece of poetry such as Coleridge's *Rime of the Ancient Mariner* where he uses the letter b to convey the drumming of the fists…

'The Wedding-Guest here beat his breast
For he heard the loud bassoon.'

Assonance

This is where a poet repeats the same vowel sound for effect. The First World War poet, Rupert Brooke, wrote a poem entitled *The Great Lover* in which he describes the things that he has loved. The long o sounds in this quotation convey the contrast between the smooth, cool sheets and the itchy quality of blankets. He tells us he has loved:

'The cool kindliness of sheets, that soon
Smooth away trouble; and the rough male kiss
Of blankets.'

Language of the senses

We know we are alive because of our five senses: we see, smell, hear, taste and touch. Poets appeal to the senses to enable us vividly to relive the experience they are describing. John Keats' beautiful *Ode to a Nightingale* captures two sensations, sight and smell, as he walks in the darkened garden and hears the nightingale,

'I cannot tell what flowers are at my feet,
Nor what soft incense hangs upon the boughs.'

Rupert Brooke reminds us of the feel of things in *The Great Lover* (see Assonance, page 75).

Walter de la Mare supplies us with the powerful sound of a horse's hoofs in *The Listeners*,

'Ay, they heard his foot upon the stirrup,
And the sound of iron on stone,
And how the silence surged softly backward
When the plunging hoofs were gone.'

We can return to Keats' *Ode to a Nightingale* for a final taste of the language of the senses as he describes the wine that he would like to drink,

'O, for a draught of vintage! That hath been
Cooled a long age in the deep-delved earth,
Tasting of Flora and the country green,
Dance, and Provençal song, and sunburnt mirth.'

We ought to point out here that Keats is not saying the wine tastes of margarine! The Flora he means are flowers.

Poetic techniques

Language can be used in two ways:

● Literal language describes writing that means word for word what it says

To say, 'he literally ran like a house on fire' is nonsense since a house on fire does not run. If you want to be literal you would have to say, 'He ran very fast'.

● Figurative language involves a comparison between what is happening and something else

The simile

The comparison can be *direct*: 'She sang like a nightingale' contains the word, *like*, and is making a direct comparison between the singer and a beautiful songbird. This is called a simile.

The metaphor

When the comparison is *implied*, it is called a metaphor as in, 'The hills are alive with the sound of music'. Tennyson is particularly skilful in the use of metaphor as he shows in *Morte d'Arthur* when Galahad walks to the lakeside as King Arthur's body is borne away into the cold dawn: 'Clothed with his breath' says the poet, capturing perfectly the icy air and the dignity of the occasion.

Personification

This is when the poet gives inanimate things the qualities of a living person. Straightforward!

'The sun smiled upon the garden.'

Imagery

Similes and metaphors are part of a wider aspect of poetic language. When the poet is making a fuller comparison, she will convey a complete picture and the name given to this is imagery:

'O, my love's like a red, red rose
that's newly sprung in June;
Oh my love's like the melody
That's sweetly sung in tune.'   (*A Red Red Rose*, Robert Burns)

In those four lines, the poet is comparing his love with a rose and a melody, both expressing beauty in their different ways – but you would note that a rose fades and an instrument goes out of tune, so you might not expect his love to last that long either. Or perhaps he didn't think of that!

A poem's message

Art represents our world and tells us more about it. A great writer sees something that she feels is true and the great poem conveys that message to the reader. The point about poetry is that it is telling us something about our world but the language it uses is always fresh and sometimes surprising. Poets use words differently, and they have rhythm and rhyme which make their words easier to remember than prose.

This is why it is especially suitable for love poetry. The man or woman tries to find new ways of describing their love, using words that will remain in the memory as proof for all time of how beautiful, powerful and true that love is.

It is interesting to compare Burns' view of love with that of the American humorist, Dorothy Parker, who is slightly more acid:

'By the time you say you're his,
Shivering and sighing
And he vows his passion is
Infinite, undying –
Lady, make a note of this:
One of you is lying.'

(*Unfortunate Coincidence*)

Different cultures and traditions

Britain is a multicultural society, with a number of ethnic minority groups all rightly treated equally by the law. The existence of different cultures and traditions within our society makes us a stronger and richer nation. We are all exposed to a wide range of food, music, art, dance, film and literature. And all of us live together in Great Britain which is a tolerant, warm society. So a part of GCSE English is devoted to studying some of the great writings from other cultures and countries. You will come across poets such as John Agard, Grace Nichols, Seamus Heaney, Moniza Alvi and, Chinua Achebe, and will be looking at the big issues that their poetry tackles, such as relationships, conflict, love and power. In a controlled assessment or exam, you will be expected to compare poems by different poets.

These will be poems you will have studied with your teacher. However, some of you may have to write about a poem you have never seen before. You may be expected to write about:

- Form and language
- Characterisation and voice
- Themes and ideas

We will now look at what the examiners expect at different levels.

3 Competent

The candidates give a personal response to poetry. They understand something about different cultures and see how the poem studied fits into the wider picture. They can pick out what the writer is trying to do and how he or she interests the reader. They can identify how writing can be used to achieve a particular effect.

2 Good

The candidates produce a sensitive response. They can analyse the particular features of a culture that produce the poem and what it will mean for its readers. They can pick out special features of the writer and how he or she uses poetic techniques to achieve effects.

1 High Level

Candidates can appreciate and analyse poetry making cross-references where it seems appropriate. They can analyse and interpret complex and sophisticated concepts within the poem and grasp its meaning. They understand what makes the poet so successful and how he or she uses language and poetic devices to convey a message.

Your teachers will go through the selections of poems that you are required to study by your examination board – there are far too many possibilities for us to cover them all here.

A sample response

Read this poem, which reflects a very different period from our own, and answer the question that follows.

My Last Duchess

That's my last Duchess painted on the wall,
Looking as if she were alive. I call
That piece a wonder, now: Fra Pandolf's hands
Worked busily a day, and there she stands.
Will't please you sit and look at her? I said
"Fra Pandolf" by design, for never read
Strangers like you that pictured countenance,
The depth and passion of its earnest glance,
But to myself they turned (since none puts by
The curtain I have drawn for you, but I)
And seemed as they would ask me, if they durst,
How such a glance came there; so, not the first
Are you to turn and ask thus. Sir, 'twas not
Her husband's presence only, called that spot
Of joy into the Duchess' cheek: perhaps
Fra Pandolf chanced to say "Her mantle laps
Over my lady's wrist too much," or "Paint
Must never hope to reproduce the faint
Half-flush that dies along her throat": such stuff
Was courtesy, she thought, and cause enough
For calling up that spot of joy. She had
A heart – how shall I say? – too soon made glad,
Too easily impressed; she liked whate'er
She looked on, and her looks went everywhere.
Sir, 'twas all one! My favour at her breast,
The dropping of the daylight in the West,
The bough of cherries some officious fool
Broke in the orchard for her, the white mule

She rode with round the terrace – all and each
Would draw from her alike the approving speech,
Or blush, at least. She thanked men, – good! but thanked
Somehow – I know not how – as if she ranked
My gift of a nine-hundred-years-old name
With anybody's gift. Who'd stoop to blame
This sort of trifling? Even had you skill
In speech – (which I have not) – to make your will
Quite clear to such an one, and say, "Just this
Or that in you disgusts me; here you miss,
Or there exceed the mark" – and if she let
Herself be lessoned so, nor plainly set
Her wits to yours, forsooth, and made excuse,
E'en then would be some stooping; and I choose
Never to stoop. Oh sir, she smiled, no doubt,
Whene'er I passed her; but who passed without
Much the same smile? This grew; I gave commands;
Then all smiles stopped together. There she stands
As if alive. Will't please you rise? We'll meet
The company below, then. I repeat,
The Count your master's known munificence
Is ample warrant that no just pretence
Of mine for dowry will be disallowed;
Though his fair daughter's self, as I avowed
At starting, is my object. Nay, we'll go
Together down, sir. Notice Neptune, though,
Taming a sea-horse, thought a rarity,
Which Claus of Innsbruck cast in bronze for me!

Robert Browning, 1842.

Question:

What impression do you form about the narrator in this poem?

In your response, you should write about:

- What you think of his feelings towards his last duchess
- The way he reveals his attitude towards life
- The use of language

Notes for a response

Summary of poem

The Duke of Ferrara is showing someone his art collection. The man he is talking to is sorting out the wedding arrangements for the Duke's next marriage. We learn about the Duke's last wife whom he has had murdered.

Background to the poem

It is based on incidents in the life of Alfonso II, Duke of Ferrara in Italy. His first wife, Lucretia, died in 1561 – after three years of marriage.

The Duke's story

He is talking about a painting of his late wife by Fra Pandolf which is so cleverly painted that it is almost lifelike. He invites the listener to look more closely at the picture. He points out that she has a 'spot/Of joy' on her face. We realise that this is not something that pleased him because she looked like this not just in her husband's presence but also for the painter – and anybody else! He thinks that she was far too easily pleased:

'…She liked whate'er
She looked on, and her looks went everywhere.'

He felt she was not treating him or his family name with the respect they deserved so, 'I gave commands'. In other words he had her murdered.

Seemingly unruffled by this revelation, he suggests they go downstairs to carry on negotiations with his listener's master, a Count whose daughter he is going to marry. As they descend the stairs he points out other pieces from his art collection, in just the same tone as he has used to discuss the picture of his last duchess.

Style

This is a dramatic monologue. It was a style used by the Victorians to present social problems and Browning wrote a number of poems of this type. Dramatic monologues have certain ingredients:

- A fictional narrator who reveals his/her character through the words spoken
- The reader being seen as a character in the drama
- Elements of a drama – the narrator is acting out the scene for the reader
- The reader has to work hard to understand what is happening and end up with a clearer picture of what is going on

What makes this such a powerful poem is that the Duke is speaking directly to us. What is more disturbing is that his conversation is so casual. He seems to have stopped in his tour of the art collection to offer a few comments about this painting which happens to be of his last wife. We feel that his wife must have been such a sweet, innocent young woman whom we would certainly have liked. His careless attitude towards her death reveals him to be the most brutal of husbands, only interested in himself and the world telling him how marvellous he is.

He is a man who loves art. This portrait is just one of a large collection. We might think that art-lovers are sensitive people yet this man is capable of supreme cruelty. The Nazis used to employ slave orchestras to play classical music for the Jews as they were marched to the gas chambers. The contrast between great art and great cruelty makes the cruelty almost unbearably inhuman.

Your response

You are now in a position to start writing. The important thing is to express your feelings about the poem. Browning is writing directly to you but in the poem, you are playing the part of a person who is arranging the next marriage of the Duke. That person might not be at all horrified by the Duke's revelations; after all, in those days women were traded like pieces of art themselves so it might not seem at all terrible that the Duke would have had this woman killed. Our view is totally different! This is something you would want to bring out in your essay. The poem also focuses on the destructiveness of jealousy and pride. In your essay, you might point to other fictional characters whose jealousy led them to extremes: Othello, for instance, kills Desdemona out of jealousy.

Organising your response

Examiners realise you are working under pressure so in a GCSE examination the question may give you a sequence to work within. If not, you have to think about how you are going to structure your response. Take a little time over this because being organised and formulating a plan will reap rewards when you start writing. With this question, you could assemble your notes under the three headings. For your convenience, there is space left below for you to enter your own notes.

- The Duke's feelings

....
....
....
....
....
....

- His attitude to his last wife

....
....
....
....
....
....

- The way Browning organises and expresses his ideas

....
....
....
....

Finally

Remember the following key points which you need to cover in any response on texts from different cultures:

- Point out what the poem tells you about the different culture or time from which it comes
- Look at the language and see how the poet is using it to influence the reader
- Work out what the poem is saying – it will have a message and you must explain what this is
- Give your own response to the poem
- At all times use quotations to support your arguments

With the study of poetry at GCSE, you are asked to make comparisons and contrasts with other poems. An obvious comparison you might make with *My Last Duchess* is with other poems where the poet is talking directly to the reader.

Top tips for progress

- **Think about the title of the poem**

- **Always read a poem aloud before you start to study it**

- **Follow the punctuation carefully – it helps to make sense of the language**

- **Look at the way the poem is laid out on the page**

- **Find out what was happening at the time when the poem was written**

- **Do not begin to write until you have read the poem at least twice**

- **You do not have to like poetry to do well in this part of the examination. There is nothing wrong in saying that you do not enjoy it, nor is there any advantage in merely saying that you do enjoy it. Whatever your final view of a poem, make sure you give your reasons!**

SHAKESPEARE

Shakespeare occupies a special place in GCSE English. He is the only writer you have to study who is mentioned by name. So there's no escape!

He gains even greater importance for some students because they will study him in GCSE English and GCSE English Literature. Depending on the examination board your school has chosen, you may have to write about Shakespeare in an examination or have to complete a piece of work in a controlled assessment.

- A study of what one or more characters contribute to the play as a whole
- A detailed study of a particular scene, showing different ways in which it might be performed and how it relates to the play as a whole
- A character study showing how the language helps to create the character and how you may be able to present him/her to the audience
- A dramatic criticism of a play presented in the theatre, on film or television
- An oral assignment in which you are questioned about a particular performance in relation to the play as a whole

Think about what the examiners are looking for.

3 Competent

Candidates are required to:

- Give a personal response to the text
- Show an understanding of the ways in which meaning is conveyed, with references to language, theme, and plot
- Show an understanding of the nature and implications of the play and its structure
- Explain why the play appeals to the audience
- Understand Shakespeare's use of language

2 Good

Candidates must show:

- A perceptive personal response
- Understanding of Shakespeare's techniques
- The ability to support their arguments by reference to the text
- The ability to analyse the play as a product of its time
- Critical ability in understanding characterisation, structure and staging
- Awareness of Shakespeare's linguistic devices

1 High Level

The very best candidates can:

- Analyse and interpret the texts and explore different interpretations
- Develop convincing analyses of Shakespeare's ideas
- Display originality of thought when considering the play's moral, philosophical or social significance
- Demonstrate originality of understanding when looking at Shakespeare's awareness of what makes his plays work with an audience
- Show how underlying patterns and details of words and images affect the audience's appreciation of the play

SHAKESPEARE

Shakespeare's theatre: the historical context

William Shakespeare (1564–1616) wrote 34 plays altogether. They can be separated into five different groups according to the subject matter and theme:

- The histories, e.g. *Henry V*
- The tragedies, e.g. *Macbeth*
- The comedies, e.g. *Twelfth Night, A Midsummer Night's Dream*
- The romances, e.g. *The Tempest*
- The problem plays (!), e.g. *The Merchant of Venice, Romeo and Juliet*

Shakespeare wrote at a time of considerable political unrest. Elizabeth I was on the throne and Britain was under constant threat from Roman Catholic enemies who wanted to restore the links with Rome that Henry VIII had severed. He depended on royal approval to survive so it is hardly surprising that he is pro-monarchy, as in *Henry V* and *Macbeth*, and anti-civil war, as in *Romeo and Juliet*.

Shakespeare wrote for a company of actors he knew so he was able to tailor the parts to suit them. Women, however, were not allowed to perform on stage – acting was regarded as a low profession unsuitable for women – so all female roles had to be played by boys.

For this reason:

- There are not all that many strong parts for women
- Very often Shakespeare ensures that the boys playing women's roles are not outshone by the older actors playing male roles by restricting most females to conversations with other females. Remember the early conversation in Romeo and Juliet (I iii) where Juliet's future is discussed in a three-way female conversation: Juliet, Lady Capulet and The Nurse.

Keep an eye open for scenes where the female is given a minor role.

The Globe Theatre

The theatre with which Shakespeare's name is chiefly associated is The Globe though he didn't move there till 1599, four or five years after he started writing. The Globe lasted until 1613 when it burned down during a performance of *Henry V*. It is worth noting the primitive state of the theatre in which Shakespeare worked:

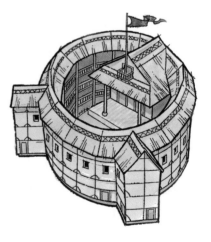

- It was open to the wind, rain and sun
- The lack of lighting meant plays had to be performed in daylight
- There was no scenery
- There was no end-of-act curtain

Such conditions encouraged the writer to be imaginative.

A single bush would represent a forest, even one as big as Birnam Wood in *Macbeth*. To convey night-time, characters would carry torches, as in *Romeo and Juliet* (I iv) when the Montague lads are on their way to the Capulets' masked ball. To indicate the end of a scene, Shakespeare would often employ a rhyming couplet, such as that used for the ending of *Julius Caesar* (V v):

'So call the field to rest, and let's away,
To part the glories of this happy day.'

Shakespeare's writing was bound by convention: plays were assumed to be in verse and were expected to follow the classical tradition. We shall consider the verse under Shakespeare's Language (see below), but there were conventions which plays were supposed to observe. The most well known of the other conventions that plays had to follow are called The Unities of Aristotle. Aristotle was a Greek dramatist who laid down certain rules that plays should follow:

- The Unity of Action – that there should be one main plot and all others should be subordinate to it
- The Unity of Place – that the play should take place at a single stage location
- The Unity of Time – that the events in the play should happen within the space of 24 hours

Shakespeare was a great writer and whilst he did observe these Unities to some degree, he was able to adapt them to his own purposes:

- **The Unity of Action:** there are other plots in *Romeo and Juliet* for example, notably the relationships between Juliet and her Nurse, and Romeo and Friar Lawrence. Paris's love for Juliet is a separate story but Paris finally becomes entangled (literally) in the love of Romeo and Juliet when he tries to stop Romeo reaching Juliet's tomb, and is killed for his trouble. His only consolation – which is not much – is that Romeo puts his dead body into Juliet's family vault

- **The Unity of Place:** you have only to think of the many different settings we have in *The Merchant of Venice* to know that Shakespeare had little time for this convention. He wanted his audiences to use their imaginations and nowhere is this stated more clearly than in the Prologue of *Henry V*:

'…Can this cockpit (the theatre) hold
The vasty fields of France? Or may we cram
Within this wooden O the very casques
That did affright the air at Agincourt?
…..
Piece out our imperfections with your thoughts
….
For 'tis your thoughts that now must deck our kings,
Carry them here and there, jumping o'er times…'

Examiner's Tip
Lay out your quotations as they are printed in the play.

- **The Unity of Time:** this is a good way of making sure we only see the climax of a story. It worked in Greek theatre but we English like to take things a bit more leisurely! After all some things do take time to happen. The events in *Romeo and Juliet* begin just after breakfast time on Sunday and the lovers have fallen in love, married, spent a night together, been separated and die – all by the early hours of Thursday morning. Matters take a little longer to sort themselves out in *Macbeth* (several months) and *The Merchant of Venice* (several weeks)

The structure of the plays

The structure of a play is the name given to the way the plot is worked out for us. Fortunately, though the stories always change, the structure in Shakespeare's plays remains the same. There are five distinct phases:

1. **The Exposition** when we are introduced to the characters and the situation. Think of the Chorus Prologue to *Romeo and Juliet* which not only tells us the situation but also reveals the ending! We have to wait till Act 1 Scene ii in Macbeth before we meet our hero and learn the witches' prophecies.

2. **The Fatal Move** (!) when one of the main characters takes a decision to do something about the situation: it can be a conscious decision – to bump off King Duncan in *Macbeth*; or an accidental one, such as when Romeo and Juliet fall in love at first sight.

3. **The Development** where the consequences of the fatal move are played out. This covers most of the middle of the play.

4. **The Crisis** that occurs when matters finally come to a head: the sword fight in *Romeo and Juliet* where Romeo kills Tybalt, and the Trial scene in *The Merchant of Venice* are examples.

5. **The Denouement or Resolution** when everything is sorted out. In Shakespeare's plays everything is sorted out. The audience doesn't go home wondering what happened to Paris, Macbeth, Shylock or Sir Toby Belch! Some are dead, others marry and the remainder end with smiles or frowns on their faces!

Shakespeare worked as an actor so he knew what worked on stage.

Shakespeare's language

This is probably the hardest part of studying the Bard!

We read all those 'thees' and 'thous' and 'haths' and 'egads' and 'gadzooks', and it all seems too difficult to follow. It is in fact an artificial difficulty since Shakespeare wrote plays to stage, not texts for GCSE examinations! The best way of understanding Shakespeare is to watch it on stage, television or film. Even audio-cassette or radio is better than wading through the pages. In that way you hear the words and though you might not understand every single one of them, you can follow the story and gradually piece together the meaning of speeches.

When you read, 'O Romeo, Romeo! Wherefore art thou Romeo?', you might be excused for thinking Juliet is actually looking for Romeo. But see the play, with the fair Juliet on her balcony wondering why on earth the hunk she fell for had to be a member of the opposing family, and there is no mistaking its meaning.

Great writing like great music is not easy. You have to read it a number of times before you begin to grasp what it is all about. And just as great music grows more and more loved with repetition, so does Shakespeare, as you see different interpretations of the play and the characters. Pop music, by the way, appeals much more quickly but you also get fed up with it more quickly too.

You need to have some idea of what Shakespeare is doing with his language. His plays are written in a mixture of prose and poetry.

Shakespearean poetry

Much of his work is written in poetry, and most of that is either blank verse or rhymed couplets. There is also the extra bonus of a sonnet every now and again!

Blank verse

Each line of verse has ten syllables, and there are five stresses in each line. Let's have a look at what that means in practice. In *Julius Caesar* (II ii), Caesar's wife Calpurnia is suggesting that he ought not to go out because of the strange omens during the night. She says,

'When beggars die, there are no comets seen'.

Count the syllables: When 1, beg 2, gars 3, die 4, there 5, are 6, no 7, com 8, ets 9, seen 10.

Now look at where the beats come in that line:

'When BEGgars DIE, there ARE no COMets SEEN'.

And there you have the classic Shakespearean line of poetry, which is also known as an iambic pentameter – the technical description for a line with five beats that goes:

di-dum di-dum di-dum di-dum di-dum.

Shakespeare is far too clever to stick to the same rhythm over and over again for he knows that repetition is boring. So he will use the basic rhythm of the line and alter it slightly to make a different point. A couple of lines after Calpurnia's warning, Caesar comes back with the famous line:

'Cowards die many times before their deaths'.

This has ten syllables but it is left to the actor to phrase it as he feels right so the rhythm is not dictated by the word arrangement. In fact, you will often hear actors deliberately changing the phrasing of a line so as to be distinct and individual in their characterisation. Juliet's speech, 'O Romeo!' is a good example, as is Hamlet's equally well known, 'To be, or not to be – that is the question' (*Hamlet* III i 56)

The important thing is that Shakespeare's verse allows the actor to find his or her own interpretation of the meaning.

Rhymed couplets (aka Heroic verse)

Simply put, this is blank verse with knobs on! It rhymes in pairs of lines. In his early plays the percentage of rhymed verse as opposed to blank verse is much higher. But rhymed verse is quite limiting and Shakespeare, as we have already discovered, did not like to have his hands tied when he was composing his plays.

The rhymed couplet has one particular use, though: to signal the end of a scene. It can neatly round off the action of a scene *and* act as a cue to the actors waiting to come on for the next scene. Look at the closing lines of *Romeo and Juliet* (V iii 309–10), and see for yourself how they complete the story:

'For never was a story of more woe
Than this of Juliet and her Romeo.'

Examiner's Tip
You can get extra credit if you show understanding of the historical context of the novel, play or poem you are studying.

The sonnet

Shakespeare wrote a large number of sonnets. They are traditionally love poems. They have fourteen lines and follow a strict rhyming pattern. *Romeo and Juliet* begins with a sonnet which is very appropriate in view of the subject matter. But Shakespeare also makes use of the sonnet more subtly in the play. When Romeo and Juliet first meet at the ball and fall in love, their conversation is structured in the form of a sonnet:

'Romeo: If I profane with my unworthiest hand
     This holy shrine, the gentle sin is this:
     My lips, two blushing pilgrims, ready stand
     To smooth that rough touch with a tender kiss.
Juliet: Good pilgrim, you do wrong your hand too much
     Which mannerly devotion shows in this;
     For saints have hands that pilgrims' hands do touch
     And palm to palm is holy palmers' kiss.
Romeo: Have not saints lips, and holy palmers too?
Juliet   Ay, pilgrim, lips that they must use in pray'r.
Romeo: Oh then, dear saint, let lips do what hands do!
     They pray: grant thou lest faith turn to despair.
Juliet: Saints do not move, though grant for prayers' sake.
Romeo: Then move not while my prayer's effect I take.'

(I v 93–106)

He kisses her and, since they have shared the sonnet, they can now beautifully and fittingly share a kiss. They are both on the same wavelength!

Shakespearean prose

Prose is everything that is not poetry.

Shakespeare often uses prose for his comic and lower-status characters. Because prose does not have the formal structure of poetry it is far more elastic and can convey all manner of ideas.

It is used in a interesting way in *Macbeth* (V i) when Lady Macbeth is observed by the Doctor and a Gentlewoman as she is sleepwalking. The two comment on her behaviour: she washes her hands trying to rid them of the blood of King Duncan. The effect of the prose is to make their conversation seem very real – concerned friends discussing another friend's illness. When she returns to her bed, the Doctor reverts to speaking in poetry, and the gravity of what they have seen is intensified by the grave lines he speaks:

'Foul whisperings are abroad, unnatural deeds
Do breed unnatural troubles; infected minds
To their deaf pillows will discharge their secrets…'

Contrasts

When you are considering Shakespeare's language, you need to weigh up a number of factors. Poetry has its beauty and its conventions and prose is generally put into the mouths of lower-status characters. But there is more to it than that. Shakespeare loved contrast, and prose contrasts strongly with poetry. Ask yourself why he has chosen to use a particular style of language in a particular situation. The answer to that question may provide you with some interesting and, in examiner-speak, 'high level' observations.

Shakespeare's characters

Shakespeare

Actors love Shakespeare. They love playing the parts because the characters are so strong. They have what is commonly referred to as three dimensions. This is rather an odd expression yet all it means is that they seem real.

Examiner's Tip
The high-level candidate can demonstrate that there is more than one way of explaining a text and can argue a preference.

Real people *are* complicated. They have characteristics that seem contradictory and thus you cannot predict how they will behave. They might be generous and open-minded about some things, but mean and narrow-minded about others. The better you know a person, the better you can understand why they behave as they do. This is true of Shakespeare's men and women.

Take *Romeo and Juliet*, for instance. Here we have a young man who falls head-over-heels in love with a lovely young woman. Well, you say, that's not unusual. Of course it isn't but he is just as crazily in love at the beginning of the play – *with a different woman*! He is so smitten that he agrees to marry this second one within hours of meeting her and asks his friend, Friar Lawrence, to conduct the ceremony. The Friar realises that Romeo is fickle and tells him so, but despite that he consents to do the honours for the young couple.

Now there are a few questions we might like to ask these two men! For a start, can Romeo really have transferred his affections so rapidly? It seems unlikely. You and I might say it's infatuation but he does actually marry Juliet, and when he finds her apparently dead in the family vault, he is so distraught that he kills himself. Surely this must be love, love at first sight, a love so powerful that he dies for his lady. His behaviour may appear unlikely but it happens and the young actor playing the part of Romeo will show that he 'loves' Rosaline (the object of his desire at the beginning) in a way that is different from the true love he feels for Juliet.

The second question we might like to put to Friar Lawrence, since he does not have the excuse of being a young man and thus behaving rashly to help his friend. He knows full well that this love Romeo is professing for Juliet is unconvincing and you might expect him to refuse to conduct the wedding ceremony. But he doesn't adopt that stance. Instead, he arranges for the marriage to happen quickly and secretly. His motives for doing this seem, on the face of it, to be quite praiseworthy: the marriage will unite two feuding families. Yet we wonder why he doesn't admit what he has done later in the play rather than arranging for Romeo to stay away from Verona and return when the coast is clear. We also wonder why the Friar does not stay with Juliet in the tomb when she awakens but runs off and leaves her to commit suicide.

We begin to realise the man is rather weak. He is very good at thinking the right things but not very good at doing them! He is, to be blunt, a coward who saves his own skin not those of the people he should be protecting.

There you have just a couple of characters whose behaviour and words offer the student food for study. The preceding paragraphs show you how to set about writing an essay on Shakespeare to a high level as it shows you have a critical ability in understanding characterisation.

As interesting in a different way is the relationship between Macbeth and his wife. Here we have a brave man whose loyal service to his king is outstanding. He meets three raddled old hags who tell him he will be King of Scotland, amongst other things. He writes to tell his wife what they have said and she immediately knows what he means. He has always been ambitious but he's been too nice a person to be ruthless in his pursuit of power. He needs her to push him into it. The opportunity arises when King Duncan comes to stay and Lady Macbeth drives her husband to murder him.

Now some people may argue that Lady Macbeth was the ambitious one: she wants him to be King so that she can be Queen. Others would say that she wants Macbeth to have what he most desires – the Scottish crown. The point is that you can find a number of different reasons why they behave as they do – and some of the reasons are contradictory.

This is exactly what a high-level candidate should do – analyse and interpret the texts and explore different interpretations.

Character development

Another aspect of Shakespeare's skill as a dramatist is his ability to draw characters that develop as the play goes on.

Macbeth begins the play as everyone's hero. His wife describes for us what she sees as a weakness, that he is 'too full of the milk of human kindness' to do what she feels needs to be done – murder the King and assume the throne.

Macbeth is persuaded by her to commit the crime but after doing so he becomes harder. He orders the murder of his best friend, Banquo, along with his son. This may be thought necessary in a twisted sort of way. Banquo knows that the Witches have prophesied a royal future for Macbeth and in such situations witnesses are dangerous. What are we to make, however, of the brutal murder of Lady Macduff and her children? This is an act of great callousness which Macbeth orders. Is he now 'too full of the milk of human kindness'? Hardly! His character has moved on.

We might also note that relationships develop as well. See how close the Macbeths are at the beginning of the play. Yet after the murder of Duncan, they begin to drift apart. Lady Macbeth knows nothing of Macbeth's part in the murder of Banquo and by the time we see her in the final act, it is clear that she is no longer intimate with her husband. It is worse than that, for when a sudden wailing is heard and Macbeth is told that his wife is dead, all he can say is 'She should have died hereafter'.

Look for other characters who develop. In *Romeo and Juliet*, both the main characters have radically altered by the time they die. The Nurse, Friar Lawrence and Lord Capulet are also changed people.

Shylock ends *The Merchant of Venice* as a defeated man, though his change of character is the most dramatic of the play. It is hard to see how the events have changed either Bassanio or Antonio, and Portia is very much the same woman we first met. By the end of the play, however, we have seen that she is quite an accomplished woman, highly intelligent and with a real gift for mimicry. It makes her love for Bassanio even more incredible!

Dramatic irony

This is one of Shakespeare's favourite dramatic devices. What it means is that he allows us, the audience, to know something crucial that is not known by the characters on stage.

In *Macbeth*, for instance, we see Banquo and Fleance out for an afternoon's ride, enjoying their time together as a typical father and son. But we know that at that very moment a gang of murderers is lying in wait to kill the pair of them. We also hear Duncan saying how nice Macbeth's castle is, yet we know that he is going to be murdered in this very place.

When Portia is defending Antonio in the Trial scene in *The Merchant of Venice*, she is disguised as a male lawyer. We know that but the characters on stage are blissfully unaware of it so we appreciate a totally different aspect of the trial.

You could say that the whole of *Romeo and Juliet* is an extended example of dramatic irony. The reason for this is that in the first lines of the play, the Prologue tells us that the young lovers are 'star-crossed' and doomed to die. None of the characters on stage knows this but Shakespeare lets us in on the story.

In all of these examples, we can read something else into Shakespeare's attitude to his audience. He treats us as privileged friends. We are a bit like God who can see everything and understand everything. We see people as if they are flies caught in a web, struggling hopelessly to avoid their fates. The effect of this is to make us feel sympathy for our fellow man.

Examiner's Tip
In a typical examination answer, you might use as many as eight quotations.

Shakespeare's themes

This is probably the most difficult aspect of understanding a Shakespearean play: knowing what it is all about. Yet it is the most important of the lot!

Is *Romeo and Juliet* about a couple of lovers who commit suicide, or is there more to it? Their love is a forbidden one, forbidden simply because they happen to have the wrong names (another very good reason for that 'Wherefore art thou Romeo?' speech). But love is blind. It takes no account of whether the person you fall for is the right person – whatever that means. In fact, as the Friar hoped, Romeo and Juliet's love does unite the families but sadly it is after their deaths which is not quite what the Friar intended.

In *Macbeth* we have a man who has a claim to the Scottish throne but takes it by murder and is himself killed. On one level it is a true tragedy – a great man comes to grief because he has a single weakness – ambition in this case. Yet on another level, it is a play of its time. Shakespeare lived in a country whose monarch was always under threat. In *Macbeth* he shows that when you are crowned king, it is the will of God and the murder of the king will not be tolerated by the Almighty.

Henry V shows us a different king – a great king who achieves greatness through his exploits in war. The point of the tale is that when Henry was a prince, he was an idle, pleasure-seeking young man but simply becoming king gave him greatness as he rose to the occasion. This is true of kings but it is also true of the rest of us. How often have we seen people who appeared weak and useless rise to the occasion when their qualities were really tested? George W. Bush lived a youth recklessly devoted to drink and self-indulgence and turned into a President who shows great powers of leadership, at least to much of the American public. Has he changed, or is he the same man with different priorities?

The Merchant of Venice is a different kettle of fish altogether. Here an idle layabout, Bassanio, borrows money from his merchant friend, Antonio, so that he can win the hand of the wealthy Portia. Antonio, however, is short of cash and gets it from a Jewish moneylender, Shylock. He in his turn has a grudge against Antonio so he imposes a strange condition: if the money is not repaid, he will be entitled to a pound of Antonio's flesh. Portia turns out to be as clever as she is beautiful and wins Antonio's case, saving him and bankrupting Shylock at the same time. What is more, by the end Bassanio gets the money and the girl!

Examiner's Tip
If the examination includes reading time, use it to plan your essay answers.

To you and me this might seem rather unfair on Shylock. When the play was written, the audience would have roared with laughter to see a Jewish enemy (for so he would be seen by the Elizabethans) defeated by a clever bunch of Christians. Nowadays we see this rather differently and some would say it was an offensively racist play. But though we may not have much time for the idle Bassanio and his very obliging friend, Antonio, we might also feel that Shylock's condition for the loan – a pound of flesh – is in fact an attempt at murder. So we could see some justice in the play's outcome.

Why is Shakespeare so highly rated?

The very fact that a man who wrote plays four hundred years ago is still studied today tells you that he must be a great writer. In fact time is the true test of greatness. The downside is that you and I cannot know who is great among contemporary writers for we shall never know if they will be remembered by generations to come.

Yet you may well ask why he has survived. There is little doubt that his poetry is of the highest quality to last so long. But it is his ideas that are greater for they concern the truth of human behaviour. We realise as we watch his plays that people have not changed, that lovers have always felt as strongly, that violent men and women have always existed, that jealousy was as ugly then as it is now.

Ours is a different world however and each generation sees a different thing in Shakespeare.

When Laurence Olivier played Henry V in the great post-war film, the audience, which had come through the Second World War saw in him a great leader bringing out the finest qualities in his fellow countrymen which they had all witnessed in this country in the fight against the Nazis.

When Romeo and Juliet fall in love against the background of a family feud, it is not hard for us to see similar stories in the modern world – Catholics and Protestants in Northern Ireland face similar difficulties, as do Muslims and Christians in some countries.

Examiner's Tip
High-level candidates have the ability to make cross-references.

Shakespeare is the most widely studied writer in the world.

In fact, you could say that each generation sees Shakespeare in a different way according to the way world events have shaped them. We in the twenty-first century interpret and perform Shakespeare's plays in a different way from previous generations because we are different people, though moved by the same things as have always moved mankind.

The greatness of Shakespeare is that his plays allow us to do just that!

How to quote from Shakespeare

The ability to use quotations is a key to improving your grade from Competent to Good! You have to support your answer by reference to the play – in other words, you have to quote! It shows you have read the play and know it well enough to use Shakespeare's words to back up your argument. First, you must learn:

The Golden Rules

1. **Quote exactly from the text.**
2. **Keep your quotations short – the shorter the better.**
3. **Lay out and punctuate them with care.**

Look at this sample paragraph from a High Level candidate and identify which of the above Golden Rules are illustrated by the underlined phrases:

The Prologue of *Romeo and Juliet* outlines the whole plot. We are told of 'Two households' whose children are 'star-crossed lovers'. The one ray of hope is that their 'death-mark'd love' is the reason for the end of their families' feud. We also learn the play will fill in the details that the Prologue has not had space to include in this sonnet:

'Which…
Is now the two-hours' traffic of our stage;
The which if you with patient ears attend,
What here shall miss, our toil shall strive to mend.'

Comment
All the quotations are exact.
All are as brief as possible.
The lengthier quotation is laid out exactly as in the text.

Top tips for progress

- **The best way to understand Shakespeare is to watch the play**

- **Prepare character studies by listing relevant quotations**

- **Work out how characters develop**

- **Note how Shakespeare uses contrast for effect**

- **Look out for dramatic irony**

- **Be sure about what the play is really saying**

PROSE

The National Curriculum allows schools to decide on the books their students will study for GCSE. It must be a range of literature from different historical times, cultures and traditions, plus a text from at least one writer on a prescribed list of pre-twentieth century writers.

Pre-twentieth century writers

It is most likely that you will have to produce a piece of work in a controlled assessment on one of the following writers, perhaps in comparison with Shakespeare. The aim is for you to understand and appreciate our rich and varied English literary heritage.

Matthew Arnold, Jane Austen, William Blake, Charlotte Brontë, Emily Brontë, Robert Browning, John Bunyan, Lord Byron, Geoffrey Chaucer, William Congreve, John Clare, Samuel Taylor Coleridge, Wilkie Collins, Joseph Conrad, Daniel Defoe, Charles Dickens, John Donne, John Dryden, George Eliot, Henry Fielding, Elizabeth Gaskell, Oliver Goldsmith, Thomas Hardy, George Herbert, Robert Herrick, Gerard Manley Hopkins, Henry James, John Keats, Christopher Marlowe, Andrew Marvell, John Milton, Alexander Pope, Mary Shelley, Percy Bysshe Shelley, RB Sheridan, Edmund Spenser, Robert Louis Stevenson, Jonathan Swift, Alfred Lord Tennyson, Anthony Trollope, Henry Vaughan, HG Wells, Oscar Wilde, William Wordsworth and Sir Thomas Wyatt

Your school may select a 'heavy' book, such as John Bunyan's *Pilgrim's Progress* or something more interesting, such as Jane Austen's *Pride and Prejudice* or *Dr Jekyll and Mr Hyde* by Robert Louis Stevenson, but it is possible to satisfy the requirements by reading several of Oscar Wilde's short stories. This section suggests ways to study Novels or Short Stories and shows you how to improve your performance in this area.

What the examiners are looking for

Here is what you have to do to succeed at different levels:

3 Competent

Candidates give a personal response to literary texts and demonstrate the ability to understand the text and the way meaning is conveyed. They understand the writer's attitudes, how the story-line develops and something about the way language is used.

2 Good

Candidates show a mature personal response, understanding the techniques used by the writer. They can analyse how a book is the product of its time and can write about a book's style, structure and characterisation.

1 High Level

Candidates have a powerful critical approach and are able to see the different ways of looking at a text. They have their own, original way of interpreting an author's work, being able to identify how a book appeals to the reader and are able to handle difficult texts with confidence and flair.

You always work best when you enjoy what you are doing. The trouble with examinations is that having to read intensively for them often spoils the enjoyment of reading itself. Hang on in there and your love of reading will return.

Of course, teachers and parents will tell you that what you really have to do is enjoy studying! Ah, how simple – but it is a lot more enjoyable if you know how to set about it.

What follows is a systematic way of looking at books so that you can tackle writing assignments with confidence and purpose.

How to read a novel

The story

The story, or plot, of a novel is a series of events that has been carefully devised by the writer to provide the best possible vehicle for ideas. Just as a Shakespearean play has its particular structure, the same is true of novels.

A typical plot may look like this:

- **Exposition** where we are told whom the story concerns, and when and where it happens
- **Complication** when the characters are challenged by a particular circumstance. Their response to this is what makes the story
- **Climax** when matters come to a head
- **Resolution** when the story ends having sorted out as much as the writer feels is necessary for the reader

A sample analysis of a text

One of the pre-twentieth century writers on the list is George Eliot. We shall work through her book *Silas Marner* under the headings given above.

Exposition: Silas comes to work as a weaver in the village of Raveloe having left his previous home after an argument over religion. Living in the village is the squire's son, Godfrey Cass, whose life is plagued by his unreliable brother, Dunstan. Godfrey has an illegitimate daughter by a local barmaid, Molly Farren.

Complication 1: Dunstan steals gold from Silas and goes missing.

Complication 2: Molly Farren dies and her daughter wanders into Silas's house. Silas adopts her, names her Eppie and brings her up as his own. Godfrey marries and watches Eppie growing up from afar.

Climax: The body of Dunstan and the missing gold are found. Godfrey finally tells his wife about Eppie, and they go to claim her from Silas.

Resolution: Ah… now that would be telling! You'll have to read it for yourself – and you'll enjoy it.

The story has been arranged so that we are watching two parallel lives: those of Silas Marner and Godfrey Cass. We quite like each of the men and the ending arrives when their two lives meet. Perhaps we might expect the one who gets what he wants at the end to be the man who has behaved better.

Q. What is the most obvious thing about a book?
A. Its title!

This is where we start. Some of the books by the prescribed authors (see above) have a single name. This is because the subjects of the earliest books were biographies and autobiographies. Charlotte Brontë wrote *Jane Eyre*; Charles Dickens wrote *David Copperfield*; and Jane Austen wrote *Emma*, all of which we can reasonably imagine will be stories about people with those names.

But where do we go with *Pride and Prejudice*?

This is about the girls in the Bennet family and there is a heroine, Elizabeth, who finally gets her man, Mr Darcy (sorry if I spoiled it for you!). It was originally called *First Impressions* but the publisher didn't think much of that as a title so *Pride and Prejudice* it became. Really it is about two people – one who suffers from pride and one who suffers from prejudice. So the title represents each of the two main characters. I won't spoil it for you this time by telling you who is which!

'Why *Silas Marner*?' is another good question since the book is about the lives of two men. Actually, George Eliot is giving us a bit of a nudge. She's really saying, 'I am more interested in Silas than Godfrey.' 'And I hope you are too,' she might have added.

Some authors use well-known quotations – or parts of them – for their titles. John Steinbeck's famous novel, *Of Mice and Men*, is part of a longer quotation from the poet Robert Burns which goes,

'The best-laid plans of mice and men
Gang aft agley'.

This is a dialect expression meaning that our best plans often go wrong. The title of the Steinbeck novel is really letting us know the ending of the story, though we do not know exactly how it will work out.

Thomas Hardy quotes directly from Thomas Gray's poem *Elegy in a Country Churchyard* describing the quiet lives led by those whose bodies are now laid to rest in this quiet graveyard – to generate the title of *Far from the Madding Crowd*.

The narrator

The person who is actually telling the story may make comments that help you to understand the message. This is more likely to be true when we have a first person narrator. All this means is that the story is told using the word, I. Occasionally in such books the story-teller will drop us a few words of wisdom that come straight from the writer. Can you recognise this quotation?

'…I was born… on a Friday, at twelve o'clock of the night. It was remarked that the clock began to strike, and I began to cry, simultaneously.'

(*David Copperfield*, Charles Dickens – Chapter 1)

Most books are told in the third person. Sometimes we follow a single character and we see the world through that person's eyes, in much the way that we live our own lives. Sometimes the writer keeps us up-to-date with several characters so that we have a god-like overview of what is happening.

Examiner's Tip
When you read a question, underline the separate parts to ensure you have a complete answer.

Generally speaking we like the people the writer wants us to like. They are the heroes and heroines who are usually rewarded for being good. Sadly, this is often not the case in real life and it's one of the reasons that people enjoy reading – because the people they like (in other words the people most like themselves!) end up happy.

It would not be a very moral story if the bad people ended up happy since it would suggest that life smiles on villains. In fiction, if you are bad, you end up unhappily; if you are good, you come up smelling of roses. This is what is called the moral equation.

Characters

We all love a story but people are always more interesting. The special talent of a writer is that she can create people for us, people who live first on the page and then, if they are brilliantly drawn, take their place in our lives.

The vital thing about a character is that he must have more than two dimensions. No one is all good or all bad. The lovely Elizabeth Bennet referred to above is sweet, intelligent, kind and has all the virtues one could imagine but she suffers from prejudice. Jane Austen draws the character of her heroine so carefully that we can see she has merits and faults – just like ourselves.

We cannot expect all the characters in a novel to be fully developed. The man who drains the pond in which the dead body of Dunstan is discovered in *Silas Marner* is there to help the story move on. If the author examined everybody who happened to come into the action of a novel he should never get the story told, so some people exist merely as names or job descriptions!

The real characters live and breathe for us. The greatest ones do something extra – they develop as people, learning as they go, modifying their behaviour and changing their attitudes – just like ourselves.

Names

Characters arrive in a story without names and are christened by the author. This seems so obvious that it is hardly worth saying, yet just spend a moment and see if the name has a meaning that may help you to understand the character's part in the story.

Go back to *Silas Marner*. He lives in the village of Raveloe which is a strange name for an English village. But George Eliot started writing the book on a holiday to Sorrento and close to the lovely Italian port of Amalfi is a beauty spot called Ravello. Is it fanciful to imagine that was the inspiration for the name? Cass is Godfrey's surname, a name that might well come from the Latin word, Casus, meaning chance. Godfrey is a man who leaves things to chance and his name provides a sort of shorthand clue for the reader.

Think of Charles Dickens and his gallery of names: Mr Gradgrind, Mr Pecksniff, Wackford Squeers…the names are certainly intended there!

When you build up a character study, a good idea is to devote a couple of pages in a spare exercise book to each and list beneath the name, what the person does and quotations that help to identify characteristics. While you're at it, think of what their name might mean and include it as part of the character study.

Character development

Real people are changed by their experiences. If they are well drawn, characters from fiction undergo similar changes. Tess in *Tess of the d'Urbervilles* starts as a beautiful innocent country girl. A wicked 'cousin' takes advantage of her and she falls pregnant. Her real love, Angel Clare (what else could he be but honest and noble with a name like that!) deserts her and she is left to fend for herself until she is finally reunited with him. She grows a little harder as the story progresses but in the final tragic scene we still see her as the lovely innocent girl who didn't deserve her fate.

She cuts such a tragically beautiful figure that she has come to represent a particular type of woman. The great figures from books are so real it is almost as if they actually lived.

Personal response

GCSE English always looks for your personal response. A personal response to a character is a very simple thing. Just ask yourself: 'Do I like or dislike this person?'

The sort of things that will probably condition your response are:

- Character's appearance
- Treatment of other people
- Treatment by other people
- Character's beliefs

A personal response to a character is as easy as that!

Examiner's Tip
Find out the date when your set book was published and discover what was happening at the time.

Setting

The setting of a book covers both where and when the events in the story take place: the actual locality and the society in which the characters live out their lives.

The Lord of the Flies takes place on a deserted island. This location is important as the author, William Golding, looked out on the playground of the school where he taught and wondered what the boys playing around out there would be like if they were all marooned on a desert island. A simple enough idea but what a masterpiece it created.

Gulliver's Travels sees our hero voyaging to various parts of the world. He discovers odd new societies and eccentric new ways of looking at life. It is of course all a big joke as he is actually describing the odd behaviour of people in England in 1726. It is hilariously funny in places: one of the saddest groups of people are the Yahoos – who are managed by a rather nasty herd of horses!

War of the Worlds is set at some time in the future. The interest here consists in having fun thinking about how the world might change in years to come. *1984* was another book set in the future (written as it happens in 1948, a date George Orwell chose to reverse to get his title). The nearest it came to predicting the future accurately was in its creation of Big Brother!

By the way, Orwell did not foresee the TV reality game show, only an ever-watchful dictator whose citizens never have privacy. Anyone misbehaving in that world would be sent to Room 101 – a room filled with all the person's worst nightmares. In the modern-day *Big Brother* the losers are sent out into a world of hysterically cheering Friday-night revellers, converted into instant celebrities.

1984 and *Gulliver's Travels* use their settings in similar ways – to make commentaries on the way societies behave.

Characters and setting

The way that characters relate to each other is very important but often the way they react to their surroundings is the key to understanding them. The island in *The Lord of the Flies* is more than just a picturesque setting where tourists go to surf and sunbathe. It is virtually a paradise and the writer is as interested in seeing how boys react to paradise as how they react to each other.

In real life too, geography affects the way a person develops. In *Wuthering Heights* we know, before we have met him, that Heathcliff is a bit of a wild character – his name tells you that. But it is almost as if he has been carved out of the wild countryside, a tempestuous, dangerous man.

Language

As elsewhere in your literary studies you will find that this is probably the most difficult aspect of a writer to analyse. For that reason demonstrating an ability in analysing language is highly rewarded in GCSE marking.

Start with the most obvious observations. The earliest forms of novel writing took the form of letter writing. This enables a character to speak directly to the reader. In Mary Shelley's *Frankenstein*, the book takes the form of a story told within letters. The writer is a man who is engaged on an exploration of the Arctic; the letters are to his sister back in England. On the journey he meets a man, Dr Frankenstein, who is hunting down the monster he has created which has turned against him. The story comes out slowly as the letter-writing continues.

Other stories are told as a series of diary entries. *Robinson Crusoe* by Daniel Defoe is a good example of this and Defoe adds to the illusion by using short note-like sentences which convey the impression of a man recording what happens as the story unfolds.

John Steinbeck's *Of Mice and Men* is an experiment in writing a play in book form. It has six chapters which are not headed as such, for they are rather like acts within a play. The opening lines of each 'chapter' resemble stage directions, giving us set, time, lighting and introducing the action:

'The bunk house was a long rectangular building…At about ten o'clock in the morning the sun threw a bright dustladen bar through one of the side windows…The wooden latch raised and a tall stoop-shouldered old man came in…'

(*Of Mice and Men*, Chapter 2)

Dialogue

Dialogue is the name given to the speech used in a novel. Since these are words actually used by a character we might expect them to tell us something about the person.

Sometimes the language will surprise us. Listen to young Helen Burns speaking about her suffering in *Jane Eyre* (Chapter 6):

'It is far better to endure patiently a smart which nobody feels but yourself, than to commit a hasty action whose evil consequences will extend to all connected with you…'

A normal child might have said something like, 'I think it's better to suffer in silence than cause trouble'. Helen Burns doesn't speak like that for very good reasons. Charlotte Brontë wants her to come across as an intelligent young girl able to make perceptive comments about life. So it is not Helen Burns speaking but Charlotte Brontë herself. She is not copying actual speech because she knows we are reading it and it gives her the chance to speak directly to her reader.

This points up a big difference between plays and novels. With a play we sit down and watch it straight through. Everything has to make sense first time. A novel can be read in any order we choose. Most of us will start at the beginning and go though in a straight line but we can stop at any moment and reread difficult bits, or go back and see what has happened. And if we are really bored, we can skip and go straight to the end and see whodunnit!

Dialogue does not usually move the plot forward at any great speed. It slows us up, often giving us a chance to understand a character's motives. Sometimes it may be used to convey tension – a short exchange of words may reveal characters acting under stress.

Sometimes it may reveal an aspect of character. Thomas Hardy has created an imaginary land for us – Wessex. It does exist in a sort of way and its people use a kind of West Country dialect. So Hardy will offer his rustics the chance to speak to us. This establishes that they are rustic and generally reveals them to be a little empty-headed and unconsciously funny.

Matthew Moon in *Far from the Madding Crowd* is talking to Gabriel Oak, a shepherd, about how limited Joseph Poorgrass (there's a name to conjure with) is by his inability to write very well:

'…ye can make sun-dials, and prent folks' names upon their waggons almost like copper-plate, with beautiful flourishes, and great long tails…Joseph Poorgrass use to prent…farmer James Everdene's waggon before you came, and 'a could never mind which way to turn the Js and Es…so you used to do them like this didn't ye, Joseph'.

Since there is never a need to include dialogue, always ask yourself:

Why does the writer use dialogue here?

The answer to that question may provide the answers that give you the analytical skills examiners look for in Good candidates.

PROSE

If you can come up with different explanations for a character's behaviour, you are displaying High Level skills.

In *Of Mice and Men*, Curley's wife comes across Lennie in the barn. He is alone and fretting about having accidentally killed his dog. She is dressed up:

'She wore her bright cotton dress and the mules with the reed ostrich feathers. Her face was made up and the little sausage curls were all in place.'

She is feeling sorry for herself and sympathetic towards Lennie in his misery. She lets him feel her hair:

'Feel aroun' there and see how sof' it is.'

Lennie does as she asks and gets carried away. She struggles and starts shouting. He puts his big hand over her mouth to quieten her. He breaks her neck.

Comment

There are several interpretations of this:

- *She is a cheap sort of woman who looks for approval from any man. She must be desperate because Lennie is slow*
- *She is a sad neglected woman who feels life has passed her by. She is stuck in the middle of nowhere and the only people who will talk to her are hired farmhands. She is too careless for her own good*
- *She is, despite everything, quite an innocent woman who does not appreciate the effect she has on men. Lennie is dangerous because he is unable to control his own actions. His silly attempt to shut her up results in a violent death. It is a terrible accident*

You would need to read the whole book to see which of those interpretations seems most likely. The sensitive reader would not see Lennie as a killer or the woman as cheap, but your ability to weigh up the evidence is what persuades the examiner of the strength of your response.

In mathematics, you can easily see why you are given credit for showing your working: how you arrived at the answer. The same is true with answers in your study of literature: *show how you reached your conclusions.*

Descriptive writing

Once again you need to ask yourself why the writer chooses to describe one thing rather than something else. This will help you to understand the writer's purpose.

In *The Lord of the Flies* William Golding produces a number of strong descriptions of the island on which the boys have crashed. By contrast, he never tells us how they actually got there, apart from suggesting there is a war and they have been shot down.

The reason for this may be that he is only interested in what happens when they get to the island, not what happened beforehand. His concern is with the possible outcome of a group of boys being left to themselves on a perfect island, so he concentrates on the island.

> *Plan your answers – that saves you repeating yourself.*

Style

All writers have their own style: the techniques and language they use to tell their stories. Work through these features and your answers will help you to form an opinion of what makes some writers so important:

- Their themes
- The settings they use for their novels
- The characters
- How they organise their stories
- The way they use dialogue and description
- Their language

Examiner's Tip
Use the internet to find out about the life of your chosen writer.

PROSE

How to read short stories

The short story is not just a novel cut down in size! It is a difficult form of writing since an author has less space in which to put across the story and ideas.

The plot

The answer booklet has enough space for any candidate to get top marks.

A short story writer has to reduce the story to a very concentrated form. Think of television adverts. They focus on a single episode in order to put across a single idea: without this product, the people in the episode would have been unhappy in some way.

The plot of a short story will have an unexpected twist that makes it all the more powerful.

In Thomas Hardy's *On the Western Circuit*, a barrister falls for a girl at a fair. She, however, is in love with someone else but is unable to read and write so that when the man writes to her, she is unable to understand. She asks her employer, a married woman, to read the letters and reply for her. Can you see what's coming? Yes, the employer falls in love with the man herself. It is a clever idea which is strong enough to make a short story but not to be the basis of a whole novel.

Characters

In a short story, the reader cannot be burdened with too many characters. The writer will focus on just two or three people and we will not be given lengthy details of their background and attitudes. Often a vital fact will be held back till the climax so as to make the ending that much more powerful.

Examiner's Tip
High-level candidates can give their own interpretations of the texts.

Setting

We do not need long descriptions of time or place. The writer will sketch in sufficient information for us to be able to form an opinion about setting.

The opening

The short story writer has not got much time to ensnare his reader! If you are not grabbed by the opening, the chances are that you will move on to something more appealing. Look at the opening sentences in this selection:

1. 'I shall never forget Tony's face. 'Twas a little round, firm, tight face with a seam here and there left by the smallpox, but not enough to hurt his looks in a woman's eye, though he had it baddish when he was a boy.'
(*Tony Kytes, the Arch-Deceiver*, Thomas Hardy)

2. 'My mother was twice married. She never spoke of her first husband, and it was only from other people that I have learnt what little I know about him.'
(*The Half Brothers*, Elizabeth Gaskell)

3. 'There were twenty-six of us – twenty-six living machines – incarcerated from morning to night in a damp basement-room, making dough for pretzels and cracknels.'
(*Twenty-six Men and a Girl*, Maxim Gorky)

4. 'Well, as I was saying, the Emperor got into bed…'
(*Napoleon and the Spectre*, Charlotte Brontë)

5. 'On glancing over my notes of the seventy-odd cases in which I have over the last eight years studied the methods of my friend, Sherlock Holmes, I find many tragic, some comic, a large number merely strange, but none commonplace…'
(*The Adventure of the Speckled Band*, Sir Arthur Conan Doyle)

This is a representative sample of quite a wide range of writers. What they have in common is immediacy. It is as though we are halfway through a conversation with the writer as we start. The Brontë extract above disposes with any pretence, 'as I was saying,' she says!

It is a technique that is calculated to secure our attention instantly. In this case, it also makes an immediate reference to the title which has persuaded us to stop at this point in the book of short stories in the first place.

Closing sentences

Can you link these five closing sentences with their openers above?

A. 'In this way I am no doubt indirectly responsible for Dr Grimesby Roylott's death, and I cannot say it is likely to weigh very heavily on my conscience.'

B. 'As before, the sun never shone into our windows – and Tanya never came to us again!'

C. 'We found a paper of directions after his death, in which he desired that he might lie at the foot of the grave, in which, by his desire, poor Gregory had been laid with his mother.'

D. 'I was not able to go to their wedding, but it was a rare party they had, by all accounts.'

E. 'The Emperor immediately fell into a fit of catalepsy, in which he continued during the whole of that night and the greater part of the next day.'

The closing sentence in a story rounds everything off. Frequently, the writer returns to the beginning and echoes the opening words or at the very least makes some reference back to them. It is a useful technique that you can use in your own writing – to glance back at the beginning as you decide how to finish your essay. If you can think of something that picks up the opening sentence you will be well rewarded! The examiner would say that your writing has coherence: that what you wrote was nicely co-ordinated!

Here by the way are the answers to the little puzzle on the previous page: 1D, 2C, 3B, 4E, 5A.

Examples of different levels of achievement

Read this passage and answer the questions set on it:

'If you know Starkfield, Massachusetts, you know the post-office. If you know the post-office you must have seen Ethan Frome drive up to it, drop the reins on his hollow-backed bay and drag himself across the brick pavement to the white colonnade: and you might have asked yourself who he was.

It was there that, several years ago, I saw him for the first time; and the sight pulled me up sharp. Even then he was the most striking figure in Starkfield, though he was but the ruin of a man. It was not so much his great height that marked him, for the 'natives' were easily singled out by their lank longitude from the stockier foreign breed: it was the careless, powerful look he had, in spite of a lameness checking each step like the jerk of a chain. There was something bleak and unapproachable in his face, and he was so stiffened and grizzled that I took him for an old man and was surprised to hear that he was not more than fifty-two. I had this from Harmon Gow, who had driven the stage from Bettsbridge to Starkfield in pre-trolley days and knew the chronicle of all the families on his line.

"He's look that way ever since he had his smash-up; and that's twenty-four years ago come next February," Harmon threw out between reminiscent pauses.'

(*Ethan Frome*, Edith Wharton – Chapter 1)

1. What impressions do you form of Ethan?
2. What methods are used to build up the picture?

3   Competent

1. Ethan is a tall man who lives in Starkfield, Massachusetts. He looks older than he is – 'I took him for an old man'. He has difficulty walking because he had an accident 24 years ago. I find him a little scary.
2. The writer describes Ethan as he drives up to the post office and says 'you might have asked yourself who he was'. He seems a very powerful man to judge from his 'striking figure'. Edith has made him very mysterious.

Comment

The candidate offers a personal response about the scariness of Frome and supports the answer with quotations which are used quite well (the last two anyway). The candidate has picked out the important things. It is not a good idea to call the writer by her Christian name!

2 Good

1. He is a tall impressive man, clearly a local Starkfielder, not one of the 'stockier foreign breed'. He walks with a pronounced limp, the result of an accident twenty-four years before. There is something rather foreboding in his appearance.

2. Edith Wharton has enjoyed herself creating this impressive man whose accident has shaped him into an almost sinister figure. His appearance is arresting for, as she says, 'you might have asked...who he was'. The language is as strong as the man, who is 'stiffened and grizzled'.

Comment

The candidate has made some strong points here, picking out key details – that he is a local for instance – and carefully quoting to secure the argument. There is a strong personal response here, that Edith Wharton 'enjoyed herself' creating this character. She may or may not have done but she has created a mysterious man whose past makes him a very intriguing figure. (By the way, calling the author Edith Wharton is a bit clumsy though better than calling her Edith.)

1 High Level

1. Ethan Frome is a memorable creation. He is a man who seems as much emotionally as physically damaged by the smash-up Harmon recalls for the narrator. He walks with difficulty and has to 'drag' himself to the post office. What is worse is that he is 'bleak and unapproachable' as if he is carrying some terrible secret.

2. Wharton conveys a sense of a remote, harsh environment. She talks to us directly almost in a familiar manner, 'If you know the post-office, you must have seen...' It's as if we already know this grim, forbidding man. We also know that he carries some dreadful secret that has made him old before his time. A 'smash-up' might damage a man badly but we feel sure that his problems are more than physical and that somehow this is the likely subject of the book, set in a town that sounds as bleak as its name: Starkfield!

Comment

This is a confident piece of writing that links Frome's physical condition with his mental state. The candidate weighs up possible interpretations about the effect of the smash-up and goes on to consider that the placing of this passage at the start of the novel may be highlighting something very significant, which may end up being the focus of the book. Sensitivity to words is also evident where the candidate picks up on the feeling of the place name, Starkfield. (Notice the High Level candidate is quite happy to call the author Wharton which suggests a professional relationship with her!)

Prose

Top tips for progress

- Read the text at least four times so that you fully know it

- Collect notes on character, setting and theme

- Find out what was happening in the world when the book was written

- Form a view of its message before you start writing

- Be sure about whom you like and dislike

- Compile key quotations with page numbers

- Read other books by the same author if you have time

SPEAKING AND LISTENING

First things first: what you have to do...

First check for yourself what each examination board requires of you in the Speaking and Listening part of your course. You need to find out from your school which examination board they are using and which Specification (or syllabus) they have chosen. However, as a general rule, the kind of tasks you will be assessed on are:

PRESENTING

Typically you may have to talk to your class about a subject or cause that interests you and then answer your classmates' or teacher's questions. Often this is done as a controlled assessment in the classroom and your teacher will be looking for your ability to communicate clearly, with a good use of language, and the ability to get your points across in an interesting and structured way. You will need to show that you can adapt your talk to suit different audiences – think of how you would change it if you were talking to a class of Year 7s for example. You may have to listen to a speech and re-present the points made.

DISCUSSING AND LISTENING

Listening is every bit as important as talking so you need to demonstrate your listening skills during group discussions. A typical task will be to work in a group and discuss how to solve a problem, such as a town planning issue. You may have to plan a presentation to your class with someone else. Listening to one another's ideas is an important part of this, and you need to demonstrate that you can work collaboratively to produce an impressive piece of work. Participating in general class discussions will help you to develop the confidence you need to do well in a controlled assessment.

ROLE PLAYING

Typically this will take the form of an interview – between a TV presenter and celebrity, a detective and suspect, or a job applicant and interviewer. Here, you will need to create convincing characters and show your ability to use appropriate language. Additionally, you should be able to show non-verbal techniques, by reacting in dramatic ways to questions or responses. Try to avoid over-acting though, unless that's what you intend! Your character needs to be believable.

So, whatever your feelings about oral work are, you are going to have to produce some good work during the course! On the positive side, what you produce is like money in the bank by the time you get to the examination itself. If you go into the examination with high achievements in the Speaking and Listening controlled assessments, you are nearly halfway to a good result!

Accent and dialect

All of us have an accent.

- Our accent is part of us. From earliest infancy, we learn to make noises by listening to the sounds made by the people around us. As we get older, we are exposed to a wider range of people and the way we pronounce words is influenced by friends, teachers, television programmes and so on. In general, we develop the accent that is most common in the region of the British Isles in which we live. If we talk to an American, he will probably conclude nothing more than that we are British, just as we can only identify a general American accent

- No accent is better than any other. They are just different

- A dialect uses different words and grammar

A Londoner might say, 'We was going to town' whilst someone from Devon would convey the same idea as 'Us be gwane to town'. In spoken English, we enjoy the differences.

When tourists descend on the remote western counties of Devon and Cornwall, the natives see them rather unflatteringly as ants and they use different words to describe these 'ants'. As we get to Devon, we become 'grockles'; forty miles further on across the Tamar, we become 'emmets'. It is a small price to pay for lovely beaches and clotted cream teas! As we sit there working out whether to put the cream on the jam or the jam on the cream, we can also enjoy being part of the West Country dialect.

Always anticipate the questions of your reader when you are giving a talk.

In the South a girl who is 'made up' is probably ready for a good night out. In the North, if you are 'made up', you are really happy about something.

Examiner's Tip
Don't fidget when you talk – it distracts your audience.

In the North, the conjunction 'while' has a different meaning from the one that is understood and accepted by the rest of the country. It means 'until'. This does not seem a very important distinction – unless you happen to be waiting at an unmanned level crossing. In the South, 'Wait while the lights are flashing' is straightforward: you sit in your car and do not move till the train has passed. In the North, they discovered that this wording was dangerous. If you wait until the lights are flashing, you will discover (if you have time to think about it) that you will move on to the crossing at the precise moment when the train is doing the same thing!

Despite the occasional misunderstanding, dialect identifies us and we should be proud of it.

When we are talking to people from our own region, it is quite acceptable to use dialect.

Idiom and slang

All languages have their own idiom. This refers to the expressions we use.

When we talk about the weather, we can say 'It's raining hard' in a number of colourful ways: 'It's raining cats and dogs' or 'It's bucketing down' are just two examples.

Slang is the sort of idiom we use in the company of people whom we know very well. It is quite expressive but we need to use it with caution as it often sounds rather rude.

'He died' is Standard English. But we all know a large number of other ways of saying the same thing: 'He kicked the bucket', 'He snuffed it' or 'He croaked his last' are pretty brutal – and slangy – ways of describing death. The best advice is to avoid slang in your Speaking and Listening assignments. It gives offence and is unnecessary!

Speaking and Listening

The extended individual contribution

The most obvious extended individual contribution is giving a talk. In this your teachers are looking for several things:

- Clear communication
- A structured talk
- Adaptability to different situations
- The use of Standard English

Some people are a pleasure to listen to. Whatever they are talking about, they are able to interest their audience and involve them in the subject matter. The film, *Kes*, offers a perfect example. Billy Casper is bullied (by his English teacher!) into talking about the only thing that really brightens his life – his kestrel. Basically, he is not that good a speaker but his teacher, Mr Farthing, supplies the audience and keeps prompting him to reveal more and more details of what fascinates him about the subject.

After a while, the boy becomes quite fluent and Mr Farthing is content to sit and listen to the talk. Billy has found a subject that fills him with enthusiasm and he has become enough of an expert to talk confidently about kestrels and how to train them.

Examiner's Tip
Using notes enables a speaker to look at his/her audience.

He starts where you must start when you are giving a talk: with a subject you know about!

Now think of the things that you know about. Such as:

- A hobby
- Your perfect playlist and what each track means to you
- Your work experience placement
- A holiday
- Animals
- An interest such as motor racing or horses
- Important events in your life
- Trips to places of interest
- A part-time job
- World problems
- Caring for others – the elderly, the sick, young children

Always speak slowly and deliberately to your audience.

The list is endless. Ideally, you want to choose as your subject something that you can do more than just talk about. If a thing really fascinates you, there will be extra material you can use in your talk. For example, talking about your kind of music would be very uninspiring if you didn't bring along some examples of the music. And, of course, a few pictures and posters will add a bit more interest for your audience.

If you are talking about a trip to a place of interest, you might draw a map for your audience's benefit so that they know how to get there. A guidebook from the place would also be an interesting object and photographs of the exhibits or attractions.

Say you want to talk about your love of horses. You might like to explain what is involved in stabling a horse. You could produce a drawing/diagram of the yard you work in; you might even bring along some of the tools and equipment you use: a saddle, a grooming kit, some rosettes you have won. The list, as someone once said, goes on!

Look around your room and see what evidence there is of the thing that interests you – the posters on the wall, the CDs you have collected, various bits and pieces you have saved which remind you of the pleasure the subject has given you.

You will need to choose the props you are going to take in to the talk with care since you don't want to arrive at the classroom weighed down like a Christmas tree. So select a few things that will add interest without distracting the audience. If you are giving a talk about a holiday, you would be foolish to take in a pile of postcards for the class to pass around as this will distract you and your classmates from the brilliant talk you have composed! A poster of the destination or a holiday souvenir would be more effective.

Preparing the talk

The subject you have chosen is:

My holiday in Sorrento

You are going to talk to the class about where you went, what you did and why they would love to go there too.

First, find a map of Italy. Choose as big a one as possible so that it can be seen comfortably from the back of the classroom. Spend some time over this as it will give the audience a clear idea of where you went. Find a friendly geography teacher (most schools have at least one!) and ask his or her advice. As a last resort, draw a large map, making it as neat and attractive as possible.

With any luck you will have kept some sort of a diary of what you did and where you went. If not, spend some time reconstructing the events of your holiday. At this stage, you will probably discover that much of your time was spent doing the same things over and over again: walking round town and looking at the different shops, going to the beach and swimming.

Select only the highlights! If you want to bore people, try describing all the details – you will soon see their eyes glaze over with excitement! So pick out only the best things:

- The boat trip to Capri
- The coach trip over the hills to Positano and Amalfi
- The coastal drive between those two places
- The trip to Pompeii
- The food – lasagne and spaghetti
- The drinks
- The weather
- The sea

When you have written down the highlights, you will begin to see that some things will take longer to describe than others and you might change your mind about the subject.

Now you come to think about it, the real highlight was the visit to Pompeii. So your subject has now become: Pompeii!

The advantage of a narrow subject is that you can focus your attention on one thing.

Your notes

The history of Pompeii

On 23 August, 79 AD Pompeii was an ordinary Roman city going about its daily life just like a hundred other cities across the Empire. Three days later, all life had been snuffed out by a massive eruption of Mount Vesuvius, killing as many as 20,000 people. Six more eruptions occur in the next five hundred years and the town sinks beneath the layers of lava till all signs of the place and its life have disappeared.

Fifteen hundred years pass till in 1594 workers, who are digging a tunnel to supply water to a nearby village, find a stone that says '*decurio Pompeiis*'. The city has been so long forgotten that most people think *Pompeiis* refers to a famous Roman general named Pompey.

In 1631 Vesuvius erupts again – the worst eruption since 79 AD. Lava flows from the volcano in seven different streams, destroying nearly all of the towns below. Another century passes before, in 1748, Spanish workers who had been excavating the buried city of Herculaneum move on to the site of Pompeii and begin digging there.

The excavations continue for over another hundred years until 1860 when Giuseppe Fiorelli is appointed as director of the Pompeiian dig. Fiorelli wants to uncover the entire Roman city. Up until this time, most people have been digging single holes or opening up small areas to look for treasure. Fiorelli wants to share the riches of the lost city with the entire world.

From 1875 onwards digging continues. Many of the objects uncovered are placed in a museum in nearby Naples, where they show the world of today much about an ancient civilisation.

Between 1913–1944 Vesuvius erupts several times, finishing the eruption cycle that started in 1631.

Today all we can see of Pompeii is ruins. But the ruins tell us many things about the ancient world. The disaster that destroyed the city of Pompeii in 79 AD preserved forever a treasury of the past. Careful excavation and exploration of the ruins continues to add to our knowledge of ancient Roman times.

Your visit

The thing that will strike you first about Pompeii is the sheer size of the place. It would take the best part of a full week to visit every street and every house, so you will have picked out just a few of the places.

The streets are still marked with ruts made by the wheels of chariots. The shops are still there as they were, getting on for two thousand years ago. They are little lock-up places lining the main streets where travellers could take refreshment or the residents could buy their food and luxuries. This was an important port in the wealthiest country on earth.

There is a huge marketplace where you can see some of the recovered pieces of architecture. It's overlooked by the volcano that still threatens the Bay of Naples and which, up until that fateful day in August, the locals had believed was nothing more deadly than a conical hill.

Your audience will enjoy walking round with you looking at the remains of the people who perished that summer's day. The people who were overcome by ash as they ran or were stifled and buried as they sheltered in bath houses or homes.

On the walls of the houses are examples of art from the time, preserved through all the years of being buried. This was a port and sailors then were little different from sailors of any age: out for a good time and a bit of fun. One such house will amuse your audience, where the local ladies provided a variety of entertainment and the walls are decorated with some extremely naughty pictures.

And so on…

The content of your talk will quickly begin to build up in your notes.

The talk

If you write the whole talk out and read it word for word, your audience will be asleep when you look up at the end!

You must make eye contact with your listeners. If that is too terrible to contemplate, pick a spot on the back wall just above the furthest head and talk to that. This keeps your voice up and ensures that your eyes are seen.

Right, you have got your subject and you have a pile of material that you are going to use as visual aids. You are going to speak to an audience in a classroom and that circumstance will affect the props you can use. *Everything has to be able to be seen from the back of the classroom.* That air ticket you needed to fly to Italy was vital but it will not be seen at the back so don't bother with it.

Far better is to pin up a large map of Italy at the front of the class so that your audience can see exactly where you went – much more interesting than how you got there!

Note making

Reduce your talk to a set of notes. Write these on to pieces of paper or card that are small enough to fit into the palm of your hand and make sure they contain sufficient prompts to keep you on track. The writing you have done on Pompeii might end up looking something like this:

People of Pompeii thought Vesuvius was a hill
Big mistake!
August 23rd 79 AD the whole lot blew up
Ash rained on the 20,000 citizens
Most were buried as they sheltered or fled
More eruptions followed in the next 500 years
City disappeared
1594 workers digging a water course find stone '*decurio Pompeiis*'
Think it's about Roman general Pompey
More eruptions
1748 a new set of diggers unearth evidence of a lost city
In 1860 Giuseppe Fiorelli takes charge of excavations
1875 a museum opened to house Pompeii exhibits
1913–44 more eruptions
Twentieth-century digs are more systematic
Pompeii is a Roman city preserved in the last moments of life
Great marketplace
Interesting houses
Places of pleasure for sailors
And so on

Number the pieces of paper carefully so that your talk remains in sequence.

Find an arresting way of starting the talk. If you grab your audience right away, you won't go wrong. A good way of starting this talk would be to say, 'Imagine all of us in this room were a few moments away from instant death and hadn't the least idea of what was about to happen…'

Then find an eye-witness account of the event. Use the internet and simply type in Pompeii or go to the website *eyewitnesstohistory.com/pompeii.htm*. This website will provide you with what you want – the Roman writer Pliny describing the events of that terrible day.

VESUVIUS

Before you start

Check you have:

- Your notes in the correct order
- Your visual aids easily available
- Dressed smartly – there is nothing worse than talking to a group of people and then discovering that you have a button, or worse, a zip (!) undone, and thinking to yourself, 'And there was me thinking they were laughing at my jokes!'

Delivering the talk

Relax and stand comfortably. This is vital. You do not want to distract your audience by fidgeting since it will unsettle them and betray your nerves.

Smile! If you are not enjoying your talk, why should they?

Speak clearly and loudly. Your audience genuinely wants to hear what you are saying.

Do not rush! The words will get lost and it is a clear sign of nerves. As a rough guide, the experienced public speaker will talk at about 100 words per minute. There will be fewer words if you are going to present visual aids. Work on the basis of about a thousand words at the most for your ten-minute talk.

Afterwards

You need to allow a few minutes to answer questions. Remember that you are the expert on Pompeii so try to prepare answers to the sort of questions that people are likely to ask:

- How much it cost to get in
- What you wore
- The need for taking water for refreshment
- What sort of souvenirs are worth bringing back…

If you don't know the answer, then admit it!

Funnily enough this is probably the point at which you can draw on the material you originally prepared when you thought you were going to talk about your holiday in Sorrento!

Different levels of performance in giving a talk

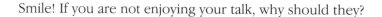

| 3 | Competent |

The candidate uses different ways of keeping the audience's interest.

| 2 | Good |

The candidate shows confidence and fluency, and is aware of the needs of the audience.

| 1 | High Level |

The candidate has the ability to gain and hold the audience by the power of his/her delivery, and can communicate complex material and ideas.

Group discussions

This is the second of the elements on which you may be assessed for oral work.

The most obvious activity under this heading is the formal debate. The word formal means following an established set of rules.

Formal debates are based on the procedures followed in the House of Commons. Think of the usual discussions you have with your friends: these are probably very shapeless affairs with everyone speaking at once, all demanding to be heard, and the loudest voice or the best looks (!) deciding whose opinion is considered the most important!

A formal debate gives everyone a chance to have his say. There is an order of speaking which is strictly followed and someone is responsible for ensuring that the rules are observed. This is as different from a normal conversation as a football match on the beach is from a premier league match!

The formal debate

Start with your proposition which will be the subject of the debate. The generally accepted pattern is for the motion, as it is called, to be expressed in formal terms:

'This house believes that school uniform is a good thing' is a typical example.

The normal procedure is to have a chairman (or chairperson if you want to be politically correct) whose job it is to ensure that the audience knows who is speaking and to ensure that no one speaks out of turn. It is easiest to have four speakers, two speaking in favour of the motion – the proposers – and two speaking against – the opposers.

The order is as follows:

1. The Chairperson introduces the motion and the speakers.
2. The Proposer of the motion presents the case outlining why school uniform is a good thing.
3. The Opposer gives the arguments against school uniform.
4. The Proposer's second speaker tries to knock down the Opposer's argument.
5. The Opposer's second tries to demolish the arguments in favour of school uniform.
6. The Chairperson invites contributions from the audience, known in a debate as The Floor.
7. The Proposer sums up the argument in favour and rallies support for his side.
8. The Opposer sums up and invites everyone to vote against the motion.
9. The Chairperson calls for a vote: those in favour, those against, abstentions.
10. The Chairperson declares the result and brings the debate to a close.

By the end hopefully all the arguments have been aired and everyone has had their say, but most of all you have enjoyed the opportunity to express your point of view and get your ideas across.

One thing you must remember is that a debate is intended to take the heat out of the argument. In the House of Commons the two front benches sit more than two sword-lengths apart. This is a quaint custom and comes from a time when parliamentary arguments could descend into open fighting!

SPEAKING AND LISTENING

In the House of Commons no one is called by name so speakers will refer to the 'Honourable Member for Salisbury' or if they are on the same political side as, 'My friend, the Member for Salisbury'. In the classroom, you must observe the same formality. Darren, who is the main speaker in favour of school uniform, is always referred to as 'The Proposer'. Amelia, who is the other main speaker, will be 'The Opposer' and so on. It may sound a bit odd but there is a good reason for it as we have shown.

Preparation of speeches

The same guidelines apply for preparing a formal speech as for giving your talk.

Put your speech in note form. This enables you to keep on the subject and more importantly to look at the audience when you speak – eye contact is vital here as it is whenever you are talking to people. If you don't look at your audience, they will think you are being untruthful and people have to believe in you in order to vote for you.

Watch how television presenters do this: their eyes will briefly flick down to their notes but they will look at you most of the time, especially when they are saying something important.

Good listening

One of the things that might strike you as strange is that this part of the examination is called Speaking and *Listening*. After all, you have to prepare talks and deliver speeches but how can you assess listening: it is simply something that we all do naturally, isn't it?

Actually listening is not natural. Remember the film we referred to earlier – when Billy Casper was talking about his kestrel? The key figure was his English teacher, Mr Farthing. It was his careful listening and well-judged questions that brought out so much of Billy's information about kestrel training.

The Good candidate has to be a good listener, and the sort of quality the examiner is looking for is sensitivity. A good listener is sensitive to the speaker's mood and feelings. You can tell this from the way he looks at the speaker, making eye contact and possibly even wearing an encouraging expression on his face. But there is another quality – shown by Mr Farthing – the ability to ask the right questions or provide an appropriate response. This can range from a murmur of appreciation to a hearty round of applause.

A High Level listener is one whose presence and response brings out the best in a speaker. You know the sort of person – looks at you directly, smiles when you express pleasure and tuts when you are displeased. And they ask exactly the right question that gets to the very heart of what you are talking about.

Different levels of performance in group activities

3   Competent

The candidate makes a number of effective contributions and listens to what others are saying.

2   Good

The candidate makes an impact on the discussion by sensitive listening and offering thought-provoking and constructive contributions.

1   High Level

The candidate listens perceptively and makes the sort of contributions that others sit up and listen to themselves!

Drama-focused activities

This, for most of us, is the most difficult of all the oral assignments we have to produce. Let's face it, few of us are born actors and very few of us actually enjoy appearing in front of an audience.

In recent years one activity has produced some really interesting work in this area: hot-seating.

Hot-seating involves a candidate attempting to play the role of a real or imaginary character and being questioned about her character, personality, motivations and life.

The standards by which candidates are judged will show you how to develop a character.

Other activities you could try are:

- Acting out a scene from your set play
- Participating in a job interview
- Making a complaint by taking a faulty piece of goods back to a shop

Your teacher, however, will dictate what you have to do and you should trust them – they know precisely what they are doing!

What the examiners are looking for in drama-focused activities:

3　Competent

The candidate creates a believable character that interests the audience by:

- Sounding like the person they are pretending to be
- Using the sort of language you might expect from that person
- Showing a convincing knowledge of the person's behaviour and actions
- Responding to questions in a detailed and convincing way

2　Good

The candidate creates a character that makes the audience sit up and listen by:

- Using a wide range of language appropriate to the person
- Tackling difficult issues in an effective way
- Responding to questions or comments in a clever and thought-provoking way

1　High Level

These candidates are like genuine actors because they are:

- Inventive
- Original and convincing
- Subtle
- Totally in control of the person they are creating

SPEAKING AND LISTENING

Examples of different levels of achievement

Task: *Imagine you are Lady Macbeth explaining your part in the play and explain your reaction to the letter Macbeth sent telling you about his meeting with the Witches*

These are extracts from the sort of responses that candidates at the different levels might give:

3   Competent

'Well, he told me that he had met three old hags on a blasted heath after a battle he had won. They told him that he would be three things: Thane of Glamis, Thane of Cawdor and King hereafter. Naturally that was interesting because I always thought he was going to be King of Scotland. He always wanted to be that. Trouble with him is that he's not tough enough. Well, not as tough as me. He needs a bit of a shove at times. Like if he's going to be King, he can't just hang around and wait for it to happen to him. And I couldn't wait for him to get back home so that I could tell him what he needed to do…'

Comment

The candidate sounds very much like the pushy wife we imagine Lady Macbeth to be, so she gets marks for being convincing. There is knowledge of the text – the details of the Witches' prophecies are conveyed. The language is a little too chatty and general: Lady Macbeth seems a bit too casual to be the sort of woman who can persuade her husband to murder the King.

2   Good

'The letter came as a bit of a shock to me. I knew he had been fighting for the King but I hardly expected to get this sort of news. I realised what it meant instantly. He said it was what was promised to me – 'greatness' he called it – but I knew that he had always wanted to be King. The trouble was that he always wanted to do it the right way. He didn't mind cheating but he was too nice a man really. I realised that the letter was my opportunity to give the man I loved what he wanted. The throne of Scotland. I couldn't wait to see him…'

Comment

Here the candidate is showing more insight into the mind of Lady Macbeth. She understands her husband and her reference to what 'he had always wanted' shows the ambitious side of Macbeth. She will help him to achieve his ambition because of her love for him. The candidate's greater knowledge of the text and the way it is conveyed add up to the 'convincing knowledge of the person's behaviour and actions' that are looked for in a Good candidate.

1 High Level

'Men! Don't you just love them! Here is my beloved man meeting a bunch of old scarecrows who tell him he is going to be King of Scotland and he's taken in by it all. How on earth will those old dears, Weird Sisters he calls them, make him King? It's the fourth old dear in his life that has the work to do! Typical male. He wants everything without having to raise a finger to get it. And it's me that has to do all the work. He'll make a lovely King and it'll be a proper reward for him. But now at last he has to do something and if he won't then I'll show him what is needed…'

Comment

Outstanding candidates have the ability to convey quite difficult ideas in a simple and compelling way. This candidate is very much a twenty-first century spokesperson: men are all very well but they need a good woman behind them to spur them on. This may or may not be what Shakespeare had in mind when he wrote the play but it is an interpretation that makes sense today. You might argue that the language is a bit informal but then again we have here a pretty tough woman describing her situation in quite blunt terms. Original, convincing and inventive are words that apply to this candidate and explain why this is High Level work.

Top tips for progress

- **Believe in yourself: nerves come from fear of failure but everyone wants you to succeed!**

- **Always use notes so that you can have eye contact with your audience**

- **Concentrate when you listen and support the speaker**

- **Learn from watching others**

- **Watch how TV newsreaders deliver their material**

- **Always speak slowly**

- **Speak as distinctly as possible**

SPELLING, PUNCTUATION AND GRAMMAR

All GCSE examination boards will award marks for good spelling, punctuation and grammar. It could make the difference to your overall grade, so it makes sense to be careful and to check your work, whether in a controlled assessment or an examination.

Spelling

If your spelling is weak, it is too late now to go back and start from the beginning. All of us have a spelling problem. The severity of it is what you might find worrying. English is a tricky language: eight out of ten words are spelt phonetically correctly. The trouble is that if you are not very good at spelling you do not know which ones are spelt as they are pronounced!

You might think you can rely on the short words. 'Dog' is all right, D-O-G – easy! But 'was' is a short word too. Mmmm… W-O-Z. No, it doesn't work!

What you need is a strategy that will enable you to learn the correct spelling of the trickiest and commonest words.

Spelling strategies

● SACAWA: this is a foolproof method which relies on repetition. It is, alas, a lengthy process and you will never have time to apply it to all the words that trouble you. But you can apply it to the words that always trouble you. All you need is a sheet of paper and a pen. Write the troublesome word (correctly!) at the top and follow this procedure. It always works. Your spelling will improve!

See the word
And
Cover the word
And
Write the word
And repeat till you get it right!

● Another strategy is to underline the difficult bit of the word. Words like 'conscience' and 'conscious' often cause problems because you can't work out what the letter c is doing there. Write out the word with 'sci' underlined – con<u>sci</u>ence and con<u>sci</u>ous. You will not forget in future

● Tricks: there are all sorts of ways of playing with words that will produce results. The word, 'rhythm', is fiendishly difficult so make it easy for yourself. What does rhythm do? Possibly…

Rhythm
Helps
You
To
Hip
Movement

SPELLING, PUNCTUATION AND GRAMMAR

● Pronunciation tricks: frequently you can learn a word simply by pronouncing it as it is written. So you would say EM-BAR-RASS-MENT and you would end up with the right number of doubled consonants. A word like 'separate' is quite easy since you will notice it has 'a rat' in it!

If all else fails, do a spell check on your computer!

● Some words give clues themselves if you look for them. Take 'stationery': is that to do with paper or something about standing still? Look carefully and notice it has 'er' in it, like paper. Easy?

● Learn the differences between homonyms (words that are spelt the same and mean different things like 'bow' and 'bow') and homophones (words that sound the same but are spelt differently like 'bow' and 'bough')

Accurate spelling does not come easily. Like every other aspect of the GCSE examination, hard work is required. But then you would not want an important examination qualification to be a piece of cake, would you?

If you really want to be an ace speller, you need to be fascinated by words.

Take 'fascinated' – why is it spelt like that? It comes from a Latin word meaning to bewitch or bind by spells. The power of the Roman state was symbolised by an axe bound in a bundle of sticks – *fasces*. This highlighted the fact that the state was more powerful because it was supported by its people. Eventually, fascinated came to mean bound…by spells. Incidentally, the same Latin word also gives us 'fascist' but that's another story…

In this test of your spelling, underline the correct word in each sentence:

1. We had a lovely dessert/desert to end the meal.
2. Her death affected/effected me badly.
3. Everyone turned up except/accept the teacher.
4. The train was stationery/stationary.
5. They're/Their/There were too/to many people there/their/they're!
6. He wrote a personnel/personal letter to his old head teacher.
7. I did not know/no whether/weather she would/wood like it.
8. The teacher was very complementary/complimentary about her pupils.
9. They where/were afraid of failure.
10. He was not aloud/allowed to play football.

Alphabet fives!

Use the SACAWA method to learn the following common and difficult words:

Absence, accommodation, address, attach, awkward

Beautiful, beginning, believe, benefit, business

Calendar, committee, conscientious, coolly, courageous

Debt, definite, disappoint, description, develop

Eerie, embarrass, environment, excellent, excite

February, forgotten, fourteen, friendly, fulfil

Gauge, geographical, grammar, grievous, guarantee

Handkerchief, harassed, height, horrible, humorous

Immediate, inconvenient, independent, instalment, irresistible

Jealousy, jewellery, judg(e)ment, ju-jitsu, junior

Keenness, kestrel, ketchup, knowledge, knowledgeable

Leisure, library, lieutenant, loneliness, loveliness

Marriage, Mediterranean, Middlesbrough, mischievous, misspelling

Necessary, neighbour, niece, ninety, nuisance

Occasion, occur, occurred, opportunity, orchestra

Pastime, parallel, parliament, possess, professor

Quaint, quarrelled, quarter, queue, queuing

Receipt, recipe, restaurant, rhythm, ridiculous

Secretary, seize, separate, sincerely, succeed

Theatre, thorough, transferred, truly, tyrant

Until, umbrella, unanimous, unique, utmost

Vegetable, vehicle, viewer, vigorous, visitor

Wednesday, weird, whole, wholly, women

Xerophagy, xylem, xylophone, x-ray, xyster (Go on, look them up!)

Yacht, yellowish, yield, ylang-ylang, yourself

Zealous, zephyr, zodiac, zoological, zucchini

Spelling answers:

1. We had a lovely dessert to end the meal.

2. Her death affected me badly.

3. Everyone turned up except the teacher.

4. The train was stationary.

5. There were too many people there!

6. He wrote a personal letter to his old head teacher.

7. I did not know whether she would like it.

8. The teacher was very complimentary about her pupils.

9. They were afraid of failure.

10. He was not allowed to play football.

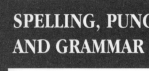

Accurate punctuation is a very difficult skill to achieve.

Most students are not quite clear about its function and most believe that in some way or another it reflects what happens when we speak. That is to say, we put a full stop where we take a breath and a comma where we pause slightly. If this were so, it would make punctuation a very random affair though, in all honesty, much written work seems to have been punctuated in this hit-or-miss spirit!

The sentence

The truth about punctuation is much simpler: it is used to make sense of writing. When we write a sentence, we begin with a capital letter and end with a full stop.

There are four types of sentence:

1. A statement: He played football.
2. A question: Did he play football?
3. An exclamation: Gosh, a footballer!
4. An order: Go and play football!

The full stop

The observant student might object that although each of the sentences above begins with a capital letter, they do not all end with a full stop. But look again. Under the exclamation mark and the question mark, there is indeed a full stop! True?

The best advice about punctuation is to think before you write. Think of what you want to write, then write it down and put the full stop. Most problems for writers occur when they are not sure of what they want to say and the sentence develops a life of its own, meandering onwards loosely until the writer runs out of puff and decides to put an end to it all by the use of a full stop or a question mark or something else like that which will indicate when the writer thinks she has said enough on the subject that she was trying to write about.

That last sentence is a pretty good example of this.

The comma

It is very tempting to pepper your writing with commas! Again, like their weightier brother, the full stop, they are used to make sense of the writing, avoiding confusion by separating ideas and expressions.

On a very simple level, they are used to separate words in a list.

'I like fish and chips and bread and marmalade.'

Written thus, it would suggest that your preference is for a plate piled high with fish, chips, bread and marmalade. This is vaguely possible though the truth is more likely to be that you like both of these pairs of food. Accordingly, you separate them with a comma.

'I like fish and chips, and bread and butter.'

Similarly, you will find that there are sentences that will be ambiguous and you can use punctuation to resolve the ambiguity for you. See the difference in meaning between these two sentences:

'Woman without her man is lost.'
'Woman – without her, man is lost!'

The colon

The colon has a couple of main uses:

● To introduce lists of things or examples
  'There are several things I want to do before I die: visit South America; ride in a hot air balloon and learn to play the piano.'

● To explain or illustrate what has come before the colon
  'I felt like death warmed up: it was the plate of mussels that had done it.'

The semi-colon

This has two main uses as well:

● To join together a series of short sentences that have much in common
  'It was early; she arose; drew back the curtains; slipped on a pair of mules, and headed for the bathroom.'

● To link together things that are introduced with a colon
  'You will need a variety of cooking utensils: a decent set of scales; a mixing bowl, and an electric mixer.'

SPELLING, PUNCTUATION AND GRAMMAR

The apostrophe

This is possibly the most difficult of all punctuation marks to use correctly. It is used in two ways:

- To indicate omission of a letter/letters
  'He doesn't know what to do'; 'It's just what I wanted.'

- To indicate possession
  'Kumar's hair was curly'; 'Kate's violin needed tuning'; 'The girls' teacher was missing.'
  In each of these cases, the apostrophe s is added to the possessor. If the possessor is already plural, we usually omit the second s.
  'The teachers' salaries were low'; 'The members' replies were treated sympathetically.'

You can adopt what sportsmen call 'the percentage approach' to the use of apostrophes. A cricketer, for instance, will find that he is most likely to be dismissed when he plays a hook shot, so he plays safe and tries not to use it!

Many people don't understand how to use apostrophes correctly. Next time you are at a greengrocer's stall in the market – one that has handwritten signs advertising its wares – you can see for yourself that apostrophes are flung with wild abandon all over the fruit and vegetables. They don't do any damage since they are not going to be entered for an English examination but they do make you feel that perhaps apostrophes are more common than you thought.

The best advice is never to use an apostrophe if you are unsure whether you need one. They are not some sort of verbal superglue for sticking an s on a word.

Examiner's Tip
If you don't know how to use the apostrophe, don't use one – you will make fewer mistakes!

Spelling, punctuation and grammar

Punctuate these sentences correctly:

1. I am my fathers son
2. what do you think youre doing
3. its my brothers cat that spilt its milk
4. were going home she said
5. now I asked do you think youre ready to start
6. itll be all right on the night
7. the kumars friends were happy to be entertained
8. this is five pounds less than I thought (Can be punctuated in two ways!)
9. did you say you liked hamlet (There are two possible meanings here too.)
10. where he had had had I had had had had had had had been correct (Now that's what I call really fiendish!)

Punctuation answers:

1. I am my father's son.
2. What do you think you're doing?
3. It's my brother's cat that spilt its milk.
4. 'We're going home,' she said.
5. 'Now,' I asked, 'do you think you're ready to start?'
6. It'll be all right on the night.
7. The Kumars' friends were happy to be entertained.
8. This is five pounds less than I thought. OR This is five pounds, less than I thought.
9. Did you say you liked Hamlet (the person)? OR Did you say you liked 'Hamlet' (the play)?
10. Where he had had 'had', I had had 'had had'. 'Had had' had been correct!

Let's be realistic, you are not going to learn grammar in the space of a few hundred words! Instead, let us have a look at the commonest errors. If you can eliminate these, you will have covered most of the important things.

Parts of speech

There are eight parts of speech, that is to say functions a word may have in a sentence: noun, pronoun, adjective, verb, adverb, preposition, conjunction and interjection.

The noun

A noun is the name of something. When there is more than one (singular), it is known as the plural. The plural is generally formed by adding an s:
Boy (singular) – Boys (plural)
There are a variety of plurals that reflect the language from which the word originally derives:
Alga-algae; axis-axes; cactus-cacti; crematorium-crematoria; criterion-criteria; die-dice; genus-genera; maestro-maestri; oasis-oases; tableau-tableaux; terminus-termini.
However tempting it may seem, never make a plural using an apostrophe!

● If you can remember the <u>1960s</u>, you could not have been alive then!

The pronoun

This replaces a noun and is used to avoid repetition. It has person and number. These are the personal pronouns used when they are the subject of a sentence:

	Singular	**Plural**
First person	I	we
Second person	you	you
Third person	he, she or it	they

● <u>She</u> and <u>I</u> went to town. Never: *Me and her went to town!*

When pronouns are used as objects, they change as follows:

	Singular	**Plural**
First person	me	us
Second person	you	you
Third person	him, her or it	them

● My mother praised <u>me</u>.

Confusion over the correct use of 'I' and 'me' is widespread. There is one school of thought that considers 'I' to be a bit posh and 'me' to be a bit common. So some people will deliberately say 'I' in order to impress others whilst another group of people are scared of being considered posh so will use 'me'.

The truth is that 'I' is correct when it is used as a subject, and 'me' is correct when used as an object or after a preposition (see below).

The adjective

This is used with a noun to indicate its qualities:

- She wore a <u>blue</u> skirt.

The verb

This is a class of word that refers to an action or state. All sentences must contain a finite verb – that is a verb with a subject.

- Mary <u>worked</u> hard.

In this sentence, Mary is the subject.

Verbs that have an object are transitive verbs, those without are intransitive.

- Jamie <u>cooked</u> a meal.

Here, the meal is the object, i.e. what Jamie cooked.

- He <u>wept</u> inconsolably.

This verb has no object.

The adverb

The adverb is used to describe the verb more precisely, indicating how, when and where a verb is done amongst other things.

- Alexis walked <u>quickly.</u> (showing how the verb, 'walked', was done)
- Kate was born <u>yesterday</u>. (showing when the verb, 'was born', was done)
- Anna stayed <u>there</u>. (showing where the verb, 'stayed', was done)

The preposition

As its name indicates, a preposition is placed before a noun to show the relationship between the noun and the rest of the sentence. Where the noun has become a pronoun, it is always used in the object case (see above).

- She stood <u>by</u> the bookcase.
- <u>Between</u> you and me, I think it is important to get it right.

(Notice how the pronouns are used!)

The conjunction

This links together two sentences, with a co-ordinating conjunction making both parts equal, and a subordinating conjunction showing how one part depends on the other.

- He worked hard <u>and</u> was highly rewarded. (a co-ordinating conjunction)
- Rosa did well <u>because</u> she worked hard. (a subordinating conjunction)

Watch for confusion between the preposition and the conjunction! 'Like' may be used as a preposition but never as a conjunction:

- No one loves you like me. (This is correct)

But if you add a verb, it becomes

- No one loves you as I do.

The interjection

There is not a lot to say about this – it simply conveys surprise or something similarly emotional.

- Cor blimey! Blooming cheek!

SPELLING, PUNCTUATION AND GRAMMAR

Standard English

Written English differs from spoken English in that it always aims to be correct English or Standard English, so that there is no room for confusion. In your GCSE coursework and written examinations, always endeavour to use your best vocabulary and express yourself as correctly as possible.

The grammar of a language is most useful to people learning it. Each language has its own idiom or way of using words. We will say, 'He kicked the bucket' and know precisely what is meant. A non-English speaker encountering the expression would be completely at a loss to understand what has happened, especially if 'he' is immediately 'carted off' to an undertaker. We cannot translate literally, i.e. word for word, from one language to another, we have to use the grammar of the language for it to make sense.

It's a pity really. If that's how it worked, all you would need to understand a foreign language would be a dictionary!

Correct these sentences:

1. The best football team won on the day.
2. No one works like she does.
3. Running up the hill, I was hit by a bus.
4. None of my friends are clever.
5. The boy done good.
6. The sprinter ran quick.
7. We was far too young to get into the pub.
8. Me and my mum was surprised by the crowd in the shop.
9. She laid down on the sofa.
10. If you practice, you will succeed.

Grammar answers:

1. The better football team won on the day.
2. No one works as she does.
3. As I was running up the hill, I was hit by a bus.
4. None of my friends is clever.
5. The boy did well.
6. The sprinter ran quickly.
7. We were far too young to get into the pub.
8. My mum and I were surprised by the crowd in the shop.
9. She lay down on the sofa.
10. If you practise, you will succeed.

- Work out why you spell words wrongly

- Adopt a strategy to tackle the difficult words

- Use your spell check regularly

- Punctuate to make sense

- Listen to good speakers to improve your speaking

- Read good books to improve your grammar

- No one notices perfect punctuation only bad punctuation.

  So make an effort to notice the punctuation when you read.

- Read your work out loud. Does it sound well-written?

- Don't litter your work with exclamation marks!

EXAMINATION PREPARATION

Examinations are scary things. When they arrive, they can stand before you like an insurmountable wall. You have been through them before in your mock exams but looking back, these seem like child's play compared to the real thing. Sometimes you will have day after day of examinations. Some may have a number of examinations in one day!

Because the size of the task is frightening, there is a danger that you will include in the list of frightening things the examiners themselves. If it is any comfort – and it probably isn't – the examiners are even more scared than you of the task that awaits them. Like you, they can see the summer holiday waiting for them but before they can roll up their jeans and paddle in a warm sea, they have hours of marking to be done.

What are examiners really like?

Examiners are teachers first and foremost. No one can make a living out of marking exam papers so this is a voluntary – but paid – service they are performing.

Remember, the examiner cannot read your mind. Make sure you get across everything you know and make your points obvious. They want to know what you know. They are not trying to catch you out and have been instructed to be as positive as possible with all the candidates' scripts they mark.

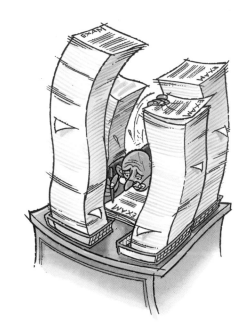

The examination boards are keen to ensure that every candidate's work is marked with complete fairness. Forget about those scare stories of vast numbers of candidates being marked down. It may happen but it is so rare that it is not worth bothering about.

There are no penalties in any marking scheme. You will never be penalised for anything you do wrongly. If your spelling, punctuation and grammar is grim, you will simply not receive the full marks that are awarded for high standards. The examiner will not slash your answer booklet with a red pen and sling it in the nearest bin!

Examiners are not allowed to go round setting their own standards. They have to follow the marking scheme.

Firstly we will look at what happens to your work after you put your pen down at the end of an examination, so you can understand the process.

The marking process

1. At the end of the examination, all the candidates' scripts are bundled up in alphabetical order and sent to an examiner.

Typically, examiners will each mark about 500 scripts in the three weeks after the examination. From the scripts they mark, a sample of about 60 will be sent to a senior examiner who will check that the marking is in line with the marking scheme, and that you have been marked neither too harshly nor too leniently. As a matter of fact, the senior examiner has his marks checked by another even more senior examiner! And so on up the line…

2. If your examiner's marking is considered to be fair, the mark for your paper will be added to the rest of the marks you achieve for the other parts of GCSE English.

If, however, the examiner appears to have been harsh or lenient, your paper will be checked again to ensure that you have received a fair mark for your work.

Only after this procedure has been observed will your final marks and the final grade be known.

3. Sometime in mid-August all the grades will be finalised and yours, along with others from your centre, will be sent back for the fateful day when you learn how well you have done.

Special circumstances

If there is anything that is likely to have had an adverse effect on your exam performance – illness or even a family bereavement – your teachers will send a covering note with your script asking for allowance to be made for this. At all times, the examination board aims to ensure you get the highest possible mark for your work.

Cheating

You, of course, would never cheat but others might attempt to do so. The examination board knows all the tricks and anyone who tries to pull a fast one will be caught. What is more, since their examination number is the same for every subject, whichever board they are taking, it is possible to disqualify all their marks for that year in every subject if a candidate has been found to be cheating.

Appeals

The examination board makes every effort to ensure that every candidate is marked fairly. If, at the end of everything, you and your teachers feel that the results are unfair, your school may appeal for your examination paper to be reconsidered. The board takes these appeals very seriously and only senior examiners are involved in re-marking papers, generally in the October following the examination.

You have to be prepared for the fact that your grade can be raised – or lowered!

Examiners' ink

This seems a rather odd aspect of marking to consider but there is a very good reason for it.

- The first time your paper is marked, it will be in red ink
- If it is reconsidered for some reason, it will be marked in green
- If a more senior examiner then has to mark your script, this will be done in purple
- The final marking – done by God himself – is in orange!

This means that you can see how your paper has been marked at different levels. The intention is always to make sure that you get the best possible mark. When you have hundreds of thousands of candidates writing answers to the same questions, you can be certain that there will be some remarkably strange answers that the Chief Examiner never thought of, so it may take three or more examiners to read them in order to see what grade they deserve.

The exam itself

The examination timetable

Before the exam season begins, the timetables are carefully worked out. Make sure you know what you are taking and when. Everyone in the country is taking the same exam at the same time, you are not allowed to take it at a different time for obvious reasons. All GCSE English examinations are timed to take place at the same time on the same day, so that you cannot enter English for two different exam boards, however much of a sucker for punishment you are!

Equipment

Make sure that you are properly equipped for the time you will spend in the examination room. Having to scratch around trying to get your pen to work will make your life very difficult. Prepare yourself an examination pack:

- Two pens, either black or blue – make sure that they are working and that they are comfortable to write with. Nothing is worse than having to scribe away for the best part of two hours with a pen that makes writing itself a chore
- A ruler
- A box of tissues!
- Some candidates like to take a lucky mascot into the room with them

Examination timing and answer booklets

The length of time allotted to an examination is carefully worked out. It is designed to give you sufficient time to:

- Read the paper
- Choose the right questions
- Make such notes as are necessary
- Write your answers
- Check through what you have written

The answer booklets you are issued with provide you with more space than you need for writing and planning as long as your handwriting is of average size. Don't be put off if you see lots of other people raising their hands to request extra sheets of paper. Unless you have very large writing, there is really enough space to do all you need to achieve the highest grades.

In fact, some of the problems in GCSE marking come from candidates writing too much! Planning your work carefully and checking the question as you write ensures that you do not write too much.

The time allowed in the examination is sufficient for the ordinary candidate to produce her best possible work. If you finish early, you have certainly missed something important, so check the questions again to see if you can spot what it is.

The average length of an essay completed in an hour under examination conditions is roughly 750 words, or three sides of paper.

Before you start writing, check how many questions you have to answer. If there are three and you have an hour and a half, spend 30 minutes on each question. Pace yourself and check the clock in the exam room to ensure you spend the appropriate amount of time on each question. If you run out of time on the first answer, leave some space and return to it later if you have time. An extra two pages on the first answer may add a couple of marks, but if you fail to do the third question at all, you will automatically lose all the marks allocated to that question.

The marks

The marks awarded for each question are printed on the examination paper. If one question is worth 10 marks and another 20 marks, you need to write twice as much for the question that is worth double the marks. If a question is worth 2 marks, don't write a page on it!

How to work in the exam room

When you are first seated, *check that you are comfortable*:

- If the sun is in your eyes,
- or the desk is rocking about,
- or there is a distracting noise
  coming from the music room, call an invigilator and complain!

When you are given your examination paper, *read it through carefully*, checking that you have read all of the pages. You may be amused by a back page that has 'This is a blank page' printed on it but this is done for your convenience in case you're worried that a question has been accidentally left out.

The examination paper will have been checked a number of times to ensure that it is completely correct. The chances of there being a mistake are virtually negligible. Nevertheless, *if there is something that strikes you as wrong*, now is the time to inform an invigilator. He may not be an English specialist so you may have to wait until one arrives.

Read the rubric carefully!

The rubric is the set of instructions to candidates telling them how many questions they have to answer and from what sections. It is a good idea to circle on the exam paper the questions you will answer.

Now focus on the first question…

How to read an examination question

The examination paper always gives you the maximum opportunity to make the best of what you know.

Here is a question from a specimen Foundation Tier paper issued by Edexcel in 2004 examination. The question concerns two poems.

'Look again at *Hide and Seek* and *Electricity Comes to Cocoa Bottom*. How does each writer enable us to share in the experiences described?

For each poem you should comment on:

- The way in which the story unfolds
- The use of words which help you to imagine the events
- The use of the senses, especially sound and sight

Support your answer with examples from the text.'

Comment
The structure of your answer is given in the question.

There are three things to consider about each poem so you will have at least six paragraphs. When you are making notes for the answer, arrange them under six headings and check that your notes actually answer the questions that are there on the paper.

The final piece of advice is to 'support your answer with examples': in other words USE QUOTATIONS! Keep them short and make sure they are relevant.

Here is a question on a selection of poems written by the poet Ted Hughes which AQA set in a past paper. It is from the Higher Tier.

'Choose two of the following features. Comment on how Hughes uses them in his poetry.

- Contrast
- Simile
- Personification

You should refer to <u>at</u> <u>least</u> <u>two</u> poems.'

Comment
This essay question has four parts. The obvious features to choose are simile and personification since they are easy to spot (provided you remember what they are of course!). The end comment is that you should 'refer to at least two poems'. That has two meanings:

1. Write about two poems.
2. Quote from both poems.

You can never over-emphasise the importance of using quotations. Where you use them, you are demonstrating that you can bring evidence from the text to support your argument. It is not enough to say, 'Ted Hughes uses a lot of similes', you must:

- *Identify them*
- *Show how they are used*

Notice that this question suggests that you refer to at least two poems. In other words, by writing about two poems you will have enough material to gain the highest marks. If the examiner thought you needed to write about three poems, she would have asked you to do that.

Just write about two poems!

EXAMINATION PREPARATION

Using an anthology

Most examination boards now use an anthology which you are given at the start of the GCSE course. For example AQA's *Moon on the Tides* is a poetry anthology, with poems selected by teachers and examiners to engage students.

The anthologies are often used in GCSE English and English Literature examinations with selections of poetry or prose on which questions are set. Most often you will be given a set poem or story in the question and you will be asked to compare it with another poem or story of your choice on a common theme from the anthology. For English Literature students you might be asked to compare it with a number of poems, not just one. Therefore it is a good idea to revise a variety of poems before you go into the exam room, then you can choose a question that allows you to write about those poems you know well. So for your revision, ask yourself:

- What is the poem/story about?
- What is the writer's background?
- What are the main themes or ideas?
- What are the unique features of the work – structure, language, voice etc?
- What are the key words, lines or sections?
- What are the key images?
- Do I like the work? Do I understand it? Can I write about it?
- How do other poems from the anthology link with this one?

The key is reading each question carefully and making the best selection for you. No doubt you will already be familiar with this sort of work throughout your course so you will know what is expected.

You will only be permitted to take in clean copies of anthologies. **No notes of any sort are permitted.**

When you quote, keep the quotations as short as possible. The examiner has a copy of the anthology as well so there is no need to waste time copying out whole paragraphs and verses. Use quotations concisely to illustrate the point you wish to make.

*Revision
tips*

EXAMINATION
PREPARATION

Section

10

Examination preparation

Make yourself a revision timetable

This is one of the best things you can do and is worth taking a little time over. List your examinations by date and time order. Think about your strengths and weaknesses. Those areas you are confident about need less revision time than those weak areas, so prioritise.

Prepare bite-size notes

When reading from a book or class notes, make bite-size notes on cards on in a notebook. You will never remember whole passages or lengthy explanations, but concise notes will trigger your memory and unlock all that information stored somewhere in your brain.

Positive Mental Attitude

It is up to you how you approach your revision. You could approach it with a negative attitude and a sense of doom, or you could think: 'Right, this is the last hurdle in a two-year journey to success. I'm going to work hard now and enjoy myself afterwards.' A positive attitude towards revision will help you to achieve your potential. And if you are prepared for an examination, you will feel much more confident when it arrives.

Get support

Sitting in a quiet room for hours looking at notes can be counter-productive. Spend an hour or two revising then enlist the help of a family member or friend to test you or listen to you as you go over what you've revised. Use online resources such as the BBC Bitesize website www.bbc.co.uk/schools/gcsebitesize/english – it's a rich source of revision material, from tests and tips to helpful videos. If you come across something that you don't understand at all, ask your teacher. They should be happy to help.

Brain Food

It may sound daft, but don't forget to eat and drink. Take a break every hour or two to refuel. Your brain and body need it.

Watch the TV

No, not *Hollyoaks*. In this digital age, you have access to an amazing archive of films and TV programmes. Watch TV adaptations or films of your set texts. Sieze the opportunity to see your set Shakespeare play on the stage – whether it is performed by the Royal Shakespeare Company or an amateur theatre group, it will help.

Get sleep

When you are asleep your brain is still active. It is busy processing all the events of the day, so if you've been revising, a good night's sleep is essential for putting all that knowledge into your memory banks. Sleep is vital for your general sense of well-being too, so if you want to be on top of your game at exam time, a good eight-hour sleep is the key.

Treat yourself

If you work to your revision timetable, you deserve regular treats. If you have done what you set out to do in a day or a week, treat yourself to a pamper evening or time on your Xbox. All hard work should be rewarded!

In the examination

- Make your handwriting as legible as possible. Your examiner is marking another 500-odd scripts so make yours neat and easy to read. Black ink is always better than blue

- Use as wide a vocabulary as you can. Difficult words are harder to spell but don't avoid them because you are frightened of making a mistake. You will get higher marks for good expression spelt wrongly than simple stuff spelt correctly!

- Keep working! All your studies have led to this point and you should not waste a moment. An examiner can see that candidates are working hard as they explore the possibilities of the questions and this does lead to higher marks

- Keep checking back on the question as you write. The commonest mistake in an examination is rambling off the subject

- Avoid the 'end of page syndrome': the feeling that something significant has happened when you have reached the end of a sheet of writing. The end of a sheet is not necessarily the end of the answer. That comes when you feel you have said enough

- If you have missed out something important, don't leave it missing. Put an asterisk where you think the missing information should go and at the end of the essay, repeat the asterisk and write the extra material. The examiner has to mark everything and she will work out where it was meant to go

- Paragraph your answers. If you forget, it is not the end of the world. You do not have to write the whole thing out all over again. Read through your answer and put a stroke between the sentences where you think a paragraph was needed, and in the margin write 'NP' – the examiner will know what you mean

When you have finished, it is too late to do anything more! Don't worry about what your friends say. You may discover that they all found it dead easy and worry that this means you must have failed.

Wrong!

You are supposed to find the exam quite difficult. That is why it brings out the best in you. You will have found it difficult because you have been answering the questions properly.

Top tips for progress

- Know your exam timetable
- Be fully equipped
- Read the question paper carefully
- Use the question to structure your answer
- Plan each answer in your answer booklet
- Time your answers carefully
- Look back at the question as you answer it to avoid rambling
- Read through your work before you hand it in

Index

Index